# IS IT TRUE?

Also by Max Cryer

# IS IT TRUE?

## The facts behind
## the things we have been told

## MAX CRYER

First published 2014

Exisle Publishing Limited,
P.O. Box 60-490, Titirangi, Auckland 0642, New Zealand.
'Moonrising', Narone Creek Road, Wollombi, NSW 2325, Australia.
www.exislepublishing.com

National Library of New Zealand Cataloguing-in-Publication Data

Cryer, Max.
Is it true? : the facts behind the things we have been told / Max Cryer.
Includes bibliographical references.
ISBN 978-1-921966-48-4
1. Questions and answers. 2. Common fallacies. I. Title.
032.02—dc 23

10 9 8 7 6 5 4 3 2 1

Text design and production by IslandBridge
Cover design by Christabella Designs
Printed in Shenzhen, China, by Ink Asia

# contents

# acknowledgements

The author thanks:

Geoffrey Pooch, Emma Sloman, Paul Barrett, Ian Watt, Graeme & Valerie Fisher, Robbie Ancel and Steve Jennings.

## Sources for illustrations

The following images are in the public domain:

- p. 17  http://commons.wikimedia.org/wiki/File:Julius_Caesar_Coustou_ Louvre_MR1798.jpg
- p. 23  http://en.wikipedia.org/wiki/File:Garden_sundial_MN_2007.JPG
- p. 88  http://en.wikipedia.org/wiki/File:John_Keats_by_William_Hilton.jpg
- p. 114  http://classicmoviechat.com/tag/garbo
- p. 122  http://simple.wikipedia.org/wiki/File:Wc0042-3b13159r.jpg
- p. 128  http://www.biostim.com.au/news/Desiderata
- p. 130  http://en.wikipedia.org/wiki/File:Robert_Bulwer_Lytton.jpg
- p. 131  http://www.victorianweb.org/art/illustration/green/2.html
- p. 132  http://www.literaryladiesguide.com/author-biography/mitchell-margaret
- p. 142  http://en.wikipedia.org/wiki/File:Great_White_Fleet.jpg
- p. 165  http://en.wikipedia.org/wiki/File:It%27s_a_Long_Way_to_ Tipperary_-_cover.JPG
- p. 187  http://en.wikipedia.org/wiki/File:Whistlers_Mother_high_res.jpg
- p. 207  King Mongkut IV: Photograph from *Mongkut, The King of Siam* by Abbot Low Moffat, Cornell University Press, 1961.
- p. 211  http://topnews.in/light/people/princess-diana

All other illustrations are from www.shutterstock.com. The following are via shutterstock:

- p. 16  <a href="http://www.shutterstock.com/gallery-1092671p1. html?cr=00&pl=edit-00">Jaguar PS</a> / <a href="http://www. shutterstock.com/?cr=00&pl=edit-00">Shutterstock.com</a>
- p. 113  <a href="http://www.shutterstock.com/gallery-751606p1. html?pl=edit-00&cr=00">Joe Seer</a> / <a href="http://www. shutterstock.com/?pl=edit-00&cr=00">Shutterstock.com</a>
- p. 196  <a href="http://www.shutterstock.com/gallery-281098p1. html?pl=edit-00&cr=00">filmfoto</a> / <a href="http://www. shutterstock.com/?pl=edit-00&cr=00">Shutterstock.com</a>

# introduction

There comes a time, somewhere towards the end of childhood, when concepts previously believed to be true are gradually revealed as illusory. It isn't Santa Claus who brings presents or the tooth fairy who leaves money under your pillow ...

But the capacity to believe survives these early reality-checks, and into adulthood many people accept what they have been told without examination. Several generations have been surrounded by advertising claims that beauty creams will banish wrinkles (they won't), that punch-n-grow hair transplanting isn't visible (it is), that a pill will make you slim (it doesn't), and that reality television shows are not contrived (they are).

But it's not just advertising. Besides the persuasive glamour that credit-card advertising offers, without ever mentioning the payments required later, the capacity to believe has stayed in place from the time Grandma passed on something she'd been told by her grandmother ... and there is a strong fibre in the human DNA to believe whatever explanation one was told first. Alas, Grandma had sometimes been given doubtful information by her own grandmother, and one thing tends to lead to another.

Many people are convinced that the Bible is the origin of Herod's stepdaughter Salome dancing with her seven veils, when actually the Bible doesn't give her any name at all — and never mentions anything about veils. The world's pre-eminent rugby trophy is called the William Webb Ellis Cup — but there is no proof that Webb Ellis had anything to do with rugby. Many people have followed what human nature tends to do: they believe what they were told first.

Sometimes a familiar concept gains several widely differing explanations over time, not one of which can be actually *proven*. Several people will tell you quite different reasons for the origin of, for example: the whole nine yards; how the word 'cocktail' came into use; no room to swing a cat; the behaviour of brass monkeys in the cold; how the word 'Yankees' came about; who was the real McCoy (or was it McKay?). These have multiple 'explanations', each of which is believed by one group of people and scorned by those who believe one of the other stories.

On another level, there are often concepts and beliefs which somehow have become misbelieved, but the original truth, when brought forward, may prove to be something of a surprise. Evidence shows that King Canute knew perfectly well that he could not command the tide. And when Queen Victoria's grand-daughter asked her when she had said 'We are not amused', Her Majesty Grandma replied that she'd never said it.

The line can be very wobbly between what we are told, what we believe, and what is the fact. Oscar Wilde wrote of Lady Bracknell: 'She is a monster without being a myth – which is rather unfair!' In the hit musical *Wizard*, author Gregory Maguire has the Wizard of Oz say: 'The truth isn't a thing of fact, or reason. It's simply what everyone agrees on.' That may be fine for a (fictional) Wizard, but not everyone thinks that way.

In 1949, American writer Dorothy M. Johnson's story 'The Man Who Shot Liberty Vallance' introduced the character of a newspaper editor whose credo was: 'If the myth gets bigger than the man, print the myth.' For the 1962 movie of Ms Johnson's story, screenwriters James Warner Bellah and Willis Goldbeck adapted her line to: 'When the legend becomes fact, print the legend.'

But some of us don't follow that credo. Printing a legend certainly doesn't make it a fact ...

# the things we say

## 'Just deserts'

*'Just deserts' means someone got what was due to them.*

Yes, it does — so long as you don't say 'desserts', or rather spell it that way when you write it down (some people do). In the real expression, 'deserts' is the noun from the verb 'to deserve', so the person should be getting what they deserve. Not 'desserts' — that's a sweet pudding.

## 'Curry favour'

*To 'curry favour' means to please someone with your cooking.*

Not at all. That curry has nothing to do with vindaloo, no matter how expert. It actually refers to curry-combing a horse ... but not just any horse: this was a fictional horse in fourteenth-century France. His name was Fauvel, and he was believed to have mystical magic powers — and also an occasional bad streak. He was owned by a French Member of Parliament, a man of considerable influence. So, to keep on the right side of the Member, there was a constant chain of people offering to curry the horse and groom him with curry-combs, to make him feel good — thus pleasing both the horse and the MP, who was inclined to show favour to people who had been attentive to the horse. Over the following hundred years, the image of the horse Fauvel being curried and groomed — resulting in good things for the groomer — drifted into English, and very conveniently the name 'Fauvel' modified into the word 'favour': to curry favour!

# OK

*'OK' is an all-American expression.*

Amidst major scholarly confusion, the origin of the expression 'OK' has been variously assigned to several different languages and dialects: French, German, Greek, Finnish, Haitian, Senegalese, Choktaw Indian, Gambian, Ligerian and Burmese. Each of those cultures has a word in their local use which they equate with 'OK'. Scottish people will say they've used it for centuries (och aye!). And there's more: besides those above, there have also been nine *other* explanations arising from various usages and abbreviations in English.

But while other cultures may say 'OK' and acknowledge its origin somewhere within their own history, the first known printing of the term in an English-speaking context was tracked down by language researcher Allen Read, who found it in the *Boston Morning Post* of March 1839. This was during a craze of the 1830s for amusing abbreviations and catchy word use — such as 'ISBD' ('it shall be done') and 'SP' ('small potatoes') — a somewhat similar practice to the use of text-message abbreviations which arose in a future century. Within that framework, the *Morning Post*'s editor, Charles Gordon Greene, wrote the article in 1839 in which he used 'OK'. It was about a jokey club called the Anti-Bell-Ringing Society ... known as ABRS. While Charles Greene's article did not explain the abbreviation ABRS, he did use the expression OK, and explained that as 'meaning *all correct*' — a deliberately jokey mis-spelling.

Soon after this first known publication, there was an American presidential election, in which it was noticed that President Van Buren had been born in a village called Kinderhook. And since he was 57 when standing for re-election, the existing expression 'OK' morphed into the nickname Old Kinderhook for Van Buren. The abbreviated version of this nickname, OK, was used as part of his presidential campaign, and a club was opened called the OK Club.

The publicity of OK being associated with Martin van Buren settled into the wider American language from 1840 onwards, meaning 'all is well'. Later, a rumour surfaced about President Van Buren's predecessor, Andrew Jackson. A scurrilous story was circulated that, since he couldn't spell properly, he had marked Presidential papers with 'O.K.' because he really thought it meant 'Orl Kurrec'. But in 2011, after meticulous research, language expert Professor Allan Metcalf published *OK: The Improbable Story of America's Greatest Word*, which presented irrefutable evidence that President Jackson, who was a qualified barrister and judge, never wrote any such thing. So 1839 nails down OK's being first seen in print in English, courtesy of Charles Gordon Greene in Boston, and from there on it blossomed through association with 'Old Kinderhook' (and not through any earlier use by earlier President Andrew Jackson).

In time, the term became firmly established in the English language worldwide, although the other claimants — France, Germany, Scotland, etc. — had been using their own version for many years before, in their languages.

So who actually invented it? Settle for the same solution as Agatha Christie did in *Murder on the Orient Express*: they all did it.

# Political correctness

> *'Political correctness' was invented by the*
> *feminist movement.*

The term came into common use during the rise of 'feminism', but its origin dates back to over a century earlier. In those earlier times there was little or no connection with careful choice of inoffensive language.

Lawyer and jurist James Wilson (appointed by President George Washington as the Supreme Court's first Associate Justice) used the term in 1793, meaning to identify that which was in line with prevailing political thought or policy:

> The states, rather than the people, for whose sake the states exist, are frequently the objects which attract and arrest our principal attention ... 'The United States,' instead of the 'People of the United States,' is the toast given. This is not politically correct.

The first recorded use in the twentieth century was in 1912 in Senator Robert La Follette's autobiography, where again he associates 'political' with 'correct' as an absolutely literal description of prevailing administrative policy: 'In those days we did not so much get correct political and economic views ...'. But a slow change was taking place, and towards the second half of the twentieth century, 'political correctness' gradually eased away from actual politics, and became the province of sensitive vocabulary.

Defined by the *Oxford English Dictionary*, 'political correctness' is:

> Conformity to a body of liberal or radical opinion, esp. on social matters, in the avoidance of anything, even established vocabulary, that may conceivably be construed as discriminatory or pejorative.

By 1986 the abbreviation 'PC' was in use and in print, and a long list of substitutions was replacing hitherto commonly used terms: Chairman became 'chairperson' or just 'the chair'; firemen became 'firefighters'; airline stewardesses were replaced by 'flight attendants'; Miss and Mrs can now both be 'Ms'; crippled became 'disabled'. Blind people are 'visually impaired'; mental retardation can be 'special needs'; Negroes are 'African Americans'; and Hispanics became 'Latino'. Total confusion reigns over Japanese, Chinese, Korean, Taiwanese and Vietnamese, who instead of their former classification as Orientals are now called 'Asians', whereas Indians, Pakistanis, Bangladeshi, Thais and Sri Lankans, who are also from Asia, are left in some sort of limbo.

The formerly common 'I now pronounce you man and wife' is sometimes replaced by the less divisive 'I now pronounce you husband and wife'. And with the growing legal acceptance of same-sex couples, gender reference can be eliminated altogether so that the decree is simply: 'I now pronounce you a married couple'. Some editions of the Bible have replaced 'brothers' with 'people', and amended 'God's right hand' to 'mighty hand' — lest 'right' offended left-handed people. The signature line from *Star Trek*, 'To boldly go where no man has gone before', was gently morphed into 'where no one has gone before'. In many circumstances 'Christmas' has been evaded — so as not to offend non-Christians — and is replaced by 'holiday', even 'holiday trees'.

With a preference for non-gender allocation, some actresses now prefer to be known as actors (which cuts their chance of an Oscar for Best Supporting Actor in half — since there would no longer be two categories!).

# SOS

*The SOS signal means 'Save Our Souls' — and the* Titanic *was the first to use it.*

'SOS' doesn't actually mean anything. It was established as an international distress signal by an agreement made between the British Marconi Society and the German Telefunk organisation at the Berlin Radio Conference, 3 October 1906.

The Morse SOS was devised as a continuous signal of three-dits-three-dahs-three-dits without any break, devised as an easy sequence to remember. The signal was formally introduced on 1 July 1908, but not actually used until nearly a year later.

The choice of signal had no intention of representing any catch-phrase, though English speakers 'interpreted' the sequence SOS as an abbreviation of 'Save Our Souls' or 'Save Our Ship'. This was creative thinking to enhance a simple sound formula. (In the German language, 'SOS' does not represent the initials of 'Save Our Souls'.)

Prior to 1908, the signal for ships in distress had been devised by the Marconi company and the call was 'CQD', which was supposed to mean 'All Stations Urgent' but was popularly misinterpreted in English as 'Come Quick — Danger' or 'Come Quickly Down'.

The first-ever radio distress signal was 'CQD', and was placed in 1899 when the merchant vessel *Elbe* ran aground on the Goodwin Sands. The message was received by the radio operator on duty at the South Foreland Lighthouse, who was able to summon the aid of the Ramsgate lifeboat.

There has long been a belief that the *Titanic* was the first vessel to use the SOS signal after it was introduced in 1908, but according to maritime researcher Patrick Robertson this is a myth. Robertson nominates the first known use of SOS three years before the sinking of the *Titanic* ... in June 1909 when the SS *Slavonia* was in distress in the North Atlantic, off the coast of Portugal.

## Dialogue

*A dialogue is when two people are talking.*

No, that's a *duo*logue. A *mono*logue is one person talking and a *dia*logue is a group of people talking — giving out information, conversing, discussing or exchanging ideas.

## Xmas

*In modern times, writing 'Xmas' is debasing the word 'Christmas'.*

Not at all, it is completely valid and not in the least disrespectful. The word 'Christ' was never part of Jesus' name — it is a title meaning 'the anointed one', or in other words 'the messiah'. In ancient Greece the letter *chi* was written with a symbol (Χ) which is very like a modern 'X', and the title assigned to Jesus — *Xristos* — was frequently abbreviated to just 'X'. So 'Xmas' can be translated as 'the mass for the anointed messiah.' The form 'Xmas' has been used in English (without disrespect) since 1551.

## Gild the lily

*The Bible tells us not to 'gild the lily'.*

Not so. An often-held impression is that the Bible says a lily is beautiful enough without any need of gilding. But the line doesn't come from the Bible, which never mentions gilding lilies. It comes close in Luke 12:27 when pointing out:

> See how the lilies of the field grow. They do not labour or spin. Yet I tell you that not even Solomon in all his splendour was dressed like one of these.

But the closer source of the common saying appears to be a modified version of Lord Salisbury's line in Shakespeare's *King John*, speaking of unnecessarily modifying that which doesn't really need it:

> To gild refined gold, to paint the lily,
> To throw a perfume on the violet,
> To smooth ice, or add another hue
> Unto the rainbow, or with taper-light
> To seek the beauteous eye of heaven to garnish,
> Is wasteful and ridiculous excess. (*King John* 4:2)

Somehow the Shakespearean image of 'painting' a lily and 'gilding' real gold became melded together in people's minds — and then associated with Luke's reporting that lilies don't toil or spin.

## Son of a bitch

*John Wayne originated the insult 'son of a bitch' in the movie* True Grit.

He may have helped make it famous, but the insult long precedes John Wayne. A version of the term was known as early as 1606 and it may have been in use earlier. But its publicly used ancestor can be found in Shakespeare's *King Lear* when the Earl of Kent describes Oswald the steward as:

> nothing but the composition of a knave, beggar, coward, pandar, and the son and heir of a mongrel bitch. (*King Lear* 2:2)

## 'Don't change horses in mid-stream'

*The expression 'Don't change horses in mid-stream' was invented by Abraham Lincoln.*

Alas, no. Mr Lincoln certainly said it in 1864 (he actually said 'it is not best to swap horses while crossing the river'), but the saying was folklore long before that, and had been in print over 20 years earlier.

The *New Hampshire Sentinel* reported on 9 February 1840 that:

> Mr. Hamer was very instrumental in bringing the meeting to his mind, by making a short speech, in the course of which he introduced the following anecdote:
>
> 'An Irishman, (said Mr. Hamer) in crossing a river in a boat, with his mare and colt, was thrown into the river, and clung to the colt's tail. The colt showed signs of exhaustion, and a man on shore told him to leave the colt and cling to the mare's tail. "Och! faith honey! this is no time to swap horses," was his reply.'

## Caesarean section

*A 'Caesarean section' birth is so called because Julius Caesar was born that way.*

There is serious doubt. The *Oxford Dictionary* (1993) covers itself by saying that the term comes 'from *the story* that Julius Caesar was so delivered'. *Encyclopedia Britannica* takes a different tack, saying that the word 'caesarean' (sometimes nowadays 'cesarean') is the name of an ancient Roman family which Pliny the Elder claimed had originated from a birth incident giving rise to the nickname *caedere/caeso* — to cut. But some believe that this also is a 'story'.

The operation of removing an unborn child by invasive surgery was certainly an acknowledged practice long before Julius. Ancient Jewish law forbade the burying of a live child within a dead mother — which would be violating the sanctity of life — so the child was excised, post-mortem. In ancient Rome, a law stated that the child of a mother dead in childbirth must be surgically removed, and similarly a woman in an extended pregnancy — say 10 months — must be delivered surgically of her baby, since it was believed she would not survive the normal birth procedure.

An emperor of India is recorded to have been born similarly c.320 BC, after his mother died in pregnancy.

Unfortunately, to modern eyes the primitive methods of surgery, infection control and dealing with haemorrhaging made it unlikely that a living pregnant woman would survive the invasive surgery, and it was extremely rare that one did.

This tends to throw further doubt on whether Julius Caesar was delivered by C-section. Not only is there no record of its having happened, but also his mother, Aurelia, who was 20 years old when Julius was born (100 BC), lived on until she was 66!

## Thomas Crapper

*The word 'crap' is derived from Thomas Crapper,*
*who invented flush toilets.*

There is no connection. The English word 'crap' (generally designated as slang) was in use 300 years before Thomas Crapper was born. It comes originally from an old French word *crape* meaning 'siftings', which moved into English as 'crappe', meaning things not wanted and discarded: chaff and trodden-on grain, weeds growing in crops, dregs from beer, and — eventually — excrement.

What's more, despite folklore, Thomas Crapper did not invent the flush toilet. Ancient civilisations had versions of them in the centuries BC. An early one in England was put together by Sir John Harrington in 1596. He made two — one for his own house, and one for his godmother, Queen Elizabeth I. Sir John called his invention the 'Ajax' — a word play on the slang term 'jakes', which meant lavatory. One legacy of his invention is that etymologists believe the slang term 'the john' originated with the sixteenth-century jocular use of his name to mean the toilet.

Although Thomas Crapper (1837–1910) did not invent the flush toilet, he did invent the ballcock mechanism system to fill the toilet tanks. His plumbing firm, Thomas Crapper and Co., did contribute a great deal to the popularity and spread of flush-toilet usage, and his name appeared on much of his manufactured product. He promoted the world's first bath, toilet and sink showroom. But the name of Thomas Crapper has no connection either with the old word 'crap' or with 'sanitary plumbing'. The name 'Crapper' is a variation of the thirteenth-century 'occupational' name Cropper.

## Decimate

*'Decimated' means 'considerable devastation'.*

Well, not exactly. The word derives from *decem*, which is Latin for '10'. When a quantity of things is 'decimated' it means that 1 out of every 10 is lost or destroyed.

## Blue blood

*Aristocratic people and royals are believed to have blue blood.*

Everyone's blood is the same colour, regardless of their social station.

The concept of special people having a special colour of blood originated in Spain as *sangre azul* — 'blue blood'. In centuries past, some areas of Spain became home to many people of Arabic or Moroccan descent, and racial mixtures produced families whose skin was darker than that of people of pure Spanish blood. Along with that, there was a resistance from rich people, especially indolent rich people, ever to expose themselves to the harsh summer sun. Spain has very hot summers, and those who had to work outdoors to keep themselves fed and housed grew to be swarthy-looking. Grandiose people didn't like this look, and went to a great deal of trouble to keep themselves out of the sun and keep their skin as pale as possible.

Skins which are very pale show the blood vessels beneath with a faintly blue tinge, but a darker skin precludes the blueness showing. Hence, Spanish people who (a) were rich enough never to have to work in the hot sun, and (b) were of pure Spanish descent, without any racial mix, were proud of their pale skin, through which faintly bluish veins showed.

So the description 'blue blood' arose in Europe to describe people of unmixed European ancestry, who did not have to work on farms or building roads. And the expression grew and widened to indicate people of a privileged class.

## Ten-gallon hat

*The name of a 10-gallon hat is self-explanatory.*

It's a nickname rather than a name ... and far from self-explanatory.

Stetson hats were originally made from beaver-fur felt which effectively repelled moisture. When Alonzo Megargee's appealing painting '*Last Drop from His Stetson*' showed a cowboy holding a Stetson hat full of water from which his horse was thirstily drinking, the image was used to advertise Stetsons from 1924 onwards. The style of hat became associated with 'cowboy culture' and movies thereof, and the expression '10-gallon hat' gradually grew from 1925. But the hats do not hold anywhere near 10 gallons and never have.

Etymologists have traced background connection with two language errors between American horsemen, and horsemen from Mexico — which caused the '10-gallon' legend. Win Blevins's *Dictionary of the American West* points out that the Spanish word for 'braid' is *galón*. Mexican *vaqueros* often decorated their Stetson hats with colourful braids, as many as 10, thus a '10 *galón*' hat, which American cowboys mis-heard as '10 gallons'. And, on the same language trail, the Mexicans sometimes referred to their decorated hats with the Spanish expression '*tan galán*'... Spanish for 'so elegant'. Again, mis-heard as '10 gallons'.

It isn't clear which of the two Mexican expressions morphed into '10 gallons' — possibly a combination of both. But either way the story absolves Stetson from advertising an untruth: the company never said that its hats held 10 gallons and, despite the nickname, the hats never did.

## His name is mud

*The saying 'His name is mud' originated in America from Dr Samuel Mudd.*

It's much older. In England the word 'mud' was being used to refer to things that were worthless or polluting as early as the 1500s. By 1700 the word had been extended to apply to people, and a low-life could be described as 'mud' — meaning a fool or a thick-skulled fellow. Over the following century, the practice of describing a useless person as 'mud' had extended to describe just the *name* of a person.

John Babcock's *Dictionary of Slang*, published in Britain in 1823, has the expression 'his name is mud'. With the association of mud as being something worthless, its being attached to someone's name indicates that the person's behaviour has caused their name to represent something not desirable or reliable.

In 1865 Abraham Lincoln was shot by a man called John Wilkes Booth, and during the incident John Booth broke a leg, which was later treated by Dr Samuel Mudd. Many people interpreted this as treasonable — since Booth was party to an assassination — and as a result of Dr Mudd helping Booth afterwards, he was initially convicted of being a conspirator. Because of this, there is a vague belief (in America) that the expression 'his name is mud' originated because of the reputation of the infamous Dr Mudd.

But alas, no. The expression 'his name is mud' had been in use in England for a long time, and was published there over 40 years before the assassination of Lincoln and before anybody had ever heard of Dr Samuel Mudd.

## The @ sign

*The @ sign is called an 'ampersand'.*

This is a fairly frequent confusion, but is not true. 'Ampersand' is the name for the sign **&**, and is not connected to @ which in English doesn't seem to have a name at all.

Italian academics explain that the symbol has been around since at least the 1500s. In those days it had a strong position in commerce, because grains and liquids were transported in jars which held a strictly measured amount. The jars were called *amphoras*, so the single letter 'a' signified goods to the weight of volume of one amphora jar, and the 'a' was written with Italian flourish — @. The sign settled to mean 'at the price of', and was used that way in Europe and other countries for centuries. For example: '3 metres of fabric @ 500 lire per metre'.

The @ sign took a while to get onto typewriter keyboards, but it was there by 1880, and by the 1960s it began to be carried over to computers. Initially, electronic messages could only be sent between users of the same computer network. A symbol was needed to be the separator in messages between different networks. American technologist Ray Tomlinson devised a way of sending messages to users of other computers, but needed an 'address' which contained a trigger that was neither a recognisable letter nor a number. He examined a keyboard and settled on the @ symbol to separate the name of the user from the 'computer address' he was using. In 1972 he sent the first message in what is now known as email, and the @ symbol took on a whole new life. It has been so successful that even languages like Tamil, Japanese and Arabic have taken it aboard, despite not using Latin alphabet letters.

But what to call it still isn't clear-cut. Most languages have their own version: Germans call it 'spider monkey'; Danish, Norwegian and Swedish alternate between calling it 'pig's tail' or 'elephant trunk'. Finns call it 'cat's tail', and in Hungarian it's 'worm'. In Israel it's called 'strudel'; French, Italians and Koreans call it a 'snail'; and in Czechoslovakia it's a word meaning 'rolled-up herring'. The Greeks call it 'little duck', and the Russians call it 'little dog.'

There are no rules about its name (except that it is not 'ampersand'). English has turned out to be the most colourless — no elephants or rolled herrings or curly-tailed monkeys. In English it is just called 'commercial at' or 'curly at'.

## Time immemorial

*'Time immemorial' is an indefinite period.*

It has drifted into meaning an indefinite period, but an ancient law actually defines the length of 'immemorial' time. It was originally entered into British law by a statute of Westminster in the year 1275. The statute decided to fix a time-limit for the bringing of certain legal actions, and that time-limit was to be the reign of King Richard I. Anything which happened *before* then was said to have happened beyond legal memory — or in 'time immemorial'. Richard I became King in 1189, so for many decades the strict meaning of the phrase time immemorial was anything before 1189. If you wanted to bring a legal action about something, it had to be something that had happened after that date.

Over the centuries, the legal aspect has faded away and the meaning has expanded somewhat, so that when people say 'since time immemorial' they mean that something has been in existence for a very long time. And when they say 'until time immemorial' they mean way into the future.

# 'Flogging a dead horse'

*'Flogging a dead horse' means pointless activity
— a horse is past its use-by date by then!*

True. But the expression seems to have crept into the language in quite a different way — namely, referring to a person who had been paid for something in advance, and then spent the proceeds unwisely. In this form, it can be found in Richard Brome's play *The Antipodes*, first performed in 1638:

> A country gentleman that fell mad — for spending of his land
>   before he sold it;
> 'Twas sold to pay his debts — all went that way for a dead horse,
>   as one would say!

There is also a strong connection with a sea-going use of the term along the same line — spending money unwisely. Admiral Smyth's very comprehensive *Sailor's Word Book* (1867) explains this as:

> When seamen ashore were engaged to be a ship's crew, before setting sail they were paid in advance for a month's work. Immediately they would spend that money.

Then when joining the ship and setting sail, for the whole of the first month the men had the (fairly unreasonable) feeling that that month's work was 'without pay' — it was a 'dead horse' month. At the end of this pre-paid month when normal wages re-start, the crew would make an effigy of a horse, drag it around the deck and cast it into the sea. The dead horse has been flogged.

Historian Alfred Simmons gives an excellent eye-witness account of exactly such a happening when he was a passenger on a sailing ship across the Pacific in 1879.

By then the expression was in use on land and in the public awareness. It surfaced in the British House of Parliament in 1859 — Hansard records the term as having been used by the Earl of Wemyss. With rather more impact, it was employed in 1867 by

MP John Bright, a renowned orator (he coined the phrase 'Britain is the mother of Parliaments'). When Parliament's dealing with the Reform Act seemed to be becoming bogged down, John Bright attempted to ignite the Members to more vigorous action by announcing that trying to get the matter activated was 'like flogging a dead horse and trying to make it pull a load'. Bright's speech, published in 1872, steered the now-common image when the term is used: that 'flogging a dead horse' refers to some project past its use-by date, or an activity which cannot result in any positive advance.

## The quick and the dead

*The 'quick and the dead' refers to those who move fast — and those who can't move at all.*

It's not quite that simple. In earlier centuries 'quick' in English meant 'alive'. It can be found as *cwice* as far back as the fourth century. Publications such as the King James Bible (1611) still use it with that meaning: 'Who shall give account to him that is ready to judge the quick and the dead' (1 Peter 4:3–5); and 'From thence he shall come to judge the quick and the dead' (the Apostles' Creed from the *Book of Common Prayer*). In both cases the reference is to judgment both on those who are living, and those who have died.

But a slow change took place over many centuries, so that the image of being 'quick, full of life, lively' became associated with speed, and gradually the word 'quick' came to mean 'fast'.

It retains its old meaning in the biblical context, as above, and in rare uses such as:

➡ the quick of a fingernail — the tender fleshy live part which supports the dead nail itself

➡ quicksand — which 'moves' as if it has life, and

➡ the first movement of a baby within a mother's womb, the 'quickening', meaning the fetus is demonstrating that it is alive.

Sometimes, the old meaning of 'quick' meaning 'alive' and the new meaning 'fast' seem to combine in a serendipitous way, such as with the 1959 western-outlaw movie *The Quick and the Dead*, which has the tagline: 'The quick and the dead — in this town you're either one or the other.'

## 'Going for a song'

*'Going for a song' means something valuable is available at a lower price.*

Curiously its historical origin was exactly the opposite.

The poem 'The Faerie Queene' was written by Elizabethan poet Edmund Spenser (left) to honour Queen Elizabeth I. Good Queen Bess was never one to swerve away from flattery, and Thomas Fuller reported in *Worthies of England* (1662) that she was so pleased with the poem that she ordered Spenser's effort be honoured in return with a gift of £100 to him, an enormous sum in the 1590s. On hearing about the Queen's wish, the Lord High Treasurer, Lord Burghley, exclaimed petulantly: 'What? All this for a song?' His remark was widely repeated and went into common usage, meaning a high payment for something of low value. Over the centuries, for no known reason, the term became both shortened and reversed in meaning — something valuable being offered at bargain price.

## 'Gone west'

*'Gone west' means broken or not working anymore — because daylight ends when the sun sets in the west.*

In its early days the expression didn't mean an unfavourable fate — quite the reverse. The expression emerged in 1851 when American journalist John Soule in Terre Haute, Indiana, wrote:

'Go West young man and grow up with the country.' In the context of the time, it was intended as a message of hope — that enterprising folk should make their way west (in the United States) as pioneers and take up a new life of promise. So he didn't mean going west was heading for failure.

'Gone west' is still in use side-by-side with newer indications of failure and disaster: 'going south' (like a sales chart where the downward line indicates falling-off growth), and 'through the floor' as opposed to 'through the roof'.

# Bimbo

*'Bimbo' is a slang term for an attractive young woman.*

Yes, in English it is; but unfortunately the word 'bimbo' actually means a young boy.

*Bimbo* is Italian, the abbreviation of the word *bambino*. The Italian language identifies the male gender by names ending in 'o' and the female by names ending in 'a' (for example, Mario and Maria). Therefore a *bambino* is a boy and a *bimbo* is a little boy — as opposed to a *bambina* a girl, and a *bimba*, a little girl.

In 1964 Jim Reeves recorded a song called 'Bimbo', which was clearly about a little boy:

Bimbo is a little boy who's got a million friends,
And every time he passes by, they all invite him in.
He'll clap his hands and sing and dance, and talk his baby talk,
With a hole in his pants and his knees a-stickin' out,
He's just big enough to walk.

The catchy refrain helped the song become an international hit, and make Reeves a star:

Bimbo, Bimbo, where ya gonna go-ee-o
Bimbo, Bimbo, whatcha gonna do-ee-o

Bimbo, Bimbo, does your mommy know
That you're goin' down the road to see a little girl-ee-o.

But somehow, at least in English-speaking countries, the word 'bimbo' crossed the gender line (somewhat to the confusion of Italians). Someone even went to the trouble of inventing the word 'himbo' to indicate a young man, seemingly unaware that 'bimbo' already meant that.

## Onanism

*'Onanism' is a polite way of saying 'masturbation'.*

The excuse for this doubtful definition is a belief that its provenance is the Holy Bible, where the reference to Onan's seed is that 'he spilled it on the ground'. However, closer examination of Genesis 38: 8–9 shows that when Onan's brother died, Judah instructed Onan to marry the widow 'and raise up seed to thy brother'. Onan did marry his brother's widow, but was aware that he could not engender a son of his brother's because any resulting child would be of his own seed. So: 'it came to pass when he went in unto his brother's wife, he spilled it on the ground'.

While 'onanism' is widely believed to be a euphemism for 'masturbation', the more logical meaning would be *coitus interruptus*.

A typically colourful Australian expression covers the same circumstance: 'Getting off at Redfern'. The Redfern train station is the last one before Sydney Central, hence taking a journey but deliberately leaving the carriage before reaching the train's ultimate destination. There is also a story told of a Londoner with a sense of humour who called his canary Onan ... because it spilled its seed upon the ground.

## 'With bated breath'

*'With baited breath' means you're waiting for something to happen and take the bait.*

It isn't 'baited' — it's 'bated', which is short for 'abated', meaning 'suppressed, becoming less in amount', such as 'By morning the storm had abated.' So 'bated breath' means less breath, suppressed breath. In other words 'holding your breath'. It's waiting with increased alertness for something to happen — but more by holding your breath rather than by 'baiting' anything.

## Awesome

*'Awesome' means you like it, and 'awful' means you hate it.*

Theoretically, they mean the same thing: 'inspiring overwhelming, admiration, or dread' — in both cases being full of awe. Over time, application of the two terms has separated to opposing ends of its meaning, so that 'awesome' is now used to mean 'inspiring admiration in the beholder' and 'awful' means 'inspiring dread in the beholder'.

## Scot-free

*'Scot-free' has the implication that Scots people are very careful with expenditure.*

Getting off 'scot-free' has nothing to do with Scotland; the term does not involve Scotland or Scottish people. In earlier centuries there was an English word in use — 'scot' — which was originally a Scandinavian word meaning 'payment'. The word was used in English as the name for a kind of British municipal tax, which was levied on people and businesses in a

proportionate way depending on values of property, etc. One way of describing the scot tax (slightly inaccurately) would be 'means test'.

In parts of Britain the tax was in force up to the 1830s. Some people who should have paid the scot were able to wiggle their way out of it and yet not break the law — what is now called 'tax avoidance'. These people were 'scot-free', and gradually the term took on a meaning of someone getting away with behaviour which was doubtful, and yet not being in any way held responsible.

## Posh

*'Posh' was how rich people sailed through the tropics — Port Out Starboard Home.*

This old 'belief' has been discounted, since nobody could find any evidence of shipping companies ever using such a booking system or the abbreviation which went with it, allowing passengers to be on the shady side of the ship during very hot areas en route. But the right characteristics of the word 'posh' as we know it were lurking in the background, already carrying a whiff of signifying 'a dandy'.

George and Weedon Grossmith's satirical serial stories *The Diary of a Nobody*, published in *Punch* in 1888–89, created characters whose names generally gave a clue to their image. One such was Murray Posh — described as 'a swell'. Then along came P.G. Wodehouse's 1903 *Tales of St. Austin's* in which he echoes university slang of the era, and has a character say:

> he wanted to know if my master allowed me to walk in the streets in that waistcoat — a remark which cut me to the quick, 'that waistcoat' being quite the most posh thing of the sort in Cambridge.

Early printing of the story used the spelling 'push' which in later editions was considered to be a misprint, and the spelling was changed to 'posh'.

By 1918, 'posh' featured in a *Punch* cartoon showing a young Air Force officer talking to his mother:

'Whatever do you mean by "posh", Gerald?'
'Don't you know? It's slang for "swish".'

And 'posh' was here to stay, meaning upper-level, polished, probably wealthy ... but without the benefit of shady cabins in a passenger ship.

Among gypsies, the Romany word for money was *posh*, which originally meant a half-penny — an unlikely ancestor to be applied to the Rothschilds or the House of Windsor.

## 'What the Dickens!'

*The saying 'What the Dickens!' must refer to Charles Dickens.*

No, it has nothing to do with Charles Dickens. At times of history with varying respect for, or reluctance to name, major figures of Christianity or Judaism, people have invented substitute terms which can't be called offensive, but everyone knows what they actually refer to. There are dozens of euphemisms for Christ and God which are considered less dramatic than saying the real word. A once-common example is 'crikey', which began to spring to international prominence in 1908 when Frank Richards invented the character of a British schoolboy called Billy Bunter, who said 'Crikey!' all the time. There were many Billy Bunter stories, and later a long-running TV series, and soon the word became very commonly used as one of many euphemisms for Christ. There's also 'cripes' for Christ, 'jeepers' and 'jumping jehosophat' and 'gee' and 'gee whiz' for Jesus. 'Drat' is short for 'God rot,' 'heck' substitutes for Hell, and God comes out as 'gosh' or 'golly'. Even 'goodness gracious' is a substitute for 'good God'.

'Dickens' is a substitute for saying Devil or Satan, so 'what the Dickens' and 'what the deuce' are actually referring to the Devil. Shakespeare uses it for one of the women in *The Merry Wives of Windsor*: 'I cannot tell what the dickens his name is.'

Sometimes 'crikey' doubles up as 'crikey dick'. This is a curious combination, since 'crikey' signifies Jesus Christ and 'dick' (short for 'Dickens') signifies the Devil ... so doubling as 'crikey dick' is more or less having a bet each way.

## 'As sure as eggs are eggs'

*'As sure as eggs are eggs' simply means that something is definite and sure.*

Yes, it does mean 'sure and definite' — and seems to have arisen from mathematics rather than poultry. In basic mathematics the symbol $x$ is taken to mean something variable and unknown. The exact configuration of $x$ must be worked out — and until then, the unknown variable remains as '$x$ is $x$'. The *sound* of this appears to have moved into vernacular speech — as 'eggs is eggs' — but in doing so has corrupted the original mathematicians' meaning. Corrupted, because it has come to mean exactly the opposite from its mathematical forbear: when something attracts the appellation 'eggs is eggs', it is being referred to as something absolutely certain, whereas '$x$ is $x$' means something unknown.

The transition from '$x$' into 'eggs' came several centuries ago, but there has been dispute about whether the poultry version (plural 'eggs') should retain the singular verb of the mathematical version ($x$ 'is' $x$). Writers have taken varied approaches to this. In 1680 a character in Thomas Otway's play *Caius Marius* speaks in dialect: "Twas to seek for Lord Marius, as sure as eggs be eggs.' Much later, Dickens's Sam Weller character (*Pickwick Papers*) in Cockney dialect, sings: 'Sure as eggs is eggs, this 'ere's the bold Turpin.' Whereas *Seinfeld*'s scriptwriter (1994) preferred the plural: 'Eggs are eggs.' So 'is' or 'are' becomes a matter of choice.

## Still waters

*'Still waters run deep.'*

This is rather selective, since if the water is truly still, a lake or a pond, it won't be running anywhere. Although Agatha Christie's Miss Marple did point out that there could be plenty of activity: 'Nothing, I believe, is so full of life under the microscope as a drop of water from a stagnant pool.' (*Murder at the Vicarage*).

## Tabloid

*'Tabloid' is an invented word describing a certain style of journalism.*

The word is from the world of patent medicines. In 1884 Henry Solomon Wellcome, of the Burroughs Wellcome pharmaceutical company, invented the word 'tabloid' to describe a new kind of medicinal tablet which was concentrated — and small.

Over a decade later, the London newspaper *Daily Mail* was launched, describing itself as 'The Busy Man's Daily Newspaper'. Its innovations included banner headlines, an economical, easily readable style, considerable sports coverage, and news specifically for women. Because the new newspaper style was compressed, compact, economical in size, with contents concentrated into an easily assimilated form, its proprietor Alfred Harmsworth referred to it in 1896 as 'tabloid' — like the Burroughs & Wellcome medicinal offerings in smaller concentrated 'tabloid' form.

The word rapidly faded from being associated with compressed medicines, and instead became firmly affixed to newspaper style. Initially it referred only to the size and accessibility of uncomplicated content, but the term slowly became associated with a particular style of 'sensational' journalism and took on a pejorative connotation.

## 'Black dog'

*Sir Winston Churchill invented the term*
*'black dog' to describe clinical depression.*

He didn't invent it. Referring to depression (or 'melancholy') as a black dog dates back to at least the 1700s. Earlier reference using the same term in the same way can also be found 50 BC in the Roman poet Horace. In 1783 Samuel Johnson referred quite frequently to his own melancholy as 'black dog', and Sir Walter Scott and Robert Louis Stevenson used the same image throughout following years.

## Grandfather clocks

*They're called 'grandfather clocks' because*
*they're tall and old.*

Their real name was (and still is) is 'long-case' clocks. But in 1876 a man wrote a song which caused the clocks to gain a new name — because of a misplaced apostrophe!

While visiting Britain in 1875, American songwriter Henry Clay Work stayed at the George Hotel in the county of Yorkshire. In the hotel, he was told about the long-case clock belonging to former owners, the Jenkins brothers. The clock's reliability began to fail when one of the Jenkins brothers died. The surviving brother lived to 90, and when he died the clock stopped completely. It never worked again, but was left standing silently in the hotel foyer. Mr Work was told the story of the silent old clock standing in the foyer, and was intrigued.

Back in America he remembered the clock which had stopped at the death of its owner, and he invented a more fanciful scenario. The Jenkins bothers were replaced by a fictional grandfather whose faithful clock had been bought on the day of his birth, had celebrated his marriage, and then stopped short, never to go again, when the old man died. Work's song 'My Grandfather's Clock' was published in 1876 and the sheet music sold over a million copies. The song became so well known that it changed the name of the (formerly called) long-case clock, but minus Mr Work's apostrophe 's'. The long-case grandfather's clock became just a 'grandfather clock', and to many people the long-case clock is still known by that name.

## 'Bunch of fives'

*'Bunch of fives' is a twentieth-century slang term.*

In spite of its contemporary sound, the expression 'bunch of fives', meaning a fist, was current in the early nineteenth century, and can be seen frequently in Pierce Egan's 1832 *Book of Sports, and Mirror of Life*. By 1837 Charles Dickens had picked it up. In *Pickwick Papers, Vol. 2*, Orson Dabbs is said to be 'shaking his bunch of fives sportively as one snaps an unloaded gun'.

## 'Significant other'

*'Significant other' was coined by Armistead Maupin to describe an unmarried partner.*

He didn't coin the term, but he helped change its earlier perception. American psychiatrist Dr Harry Stack Sullivan used the term in his 1953 book, *The Interpersonal Theory of Psychiatry*, a study of the relationship network of which an individual is the centre.

He commented on situations which may cause 'the emotional disturbance of the significant other'. At the time his use of the term signified a sibling, fiancé/ée, parent, spouse, other family relation, or business colleague — any person who held importance in another person's life.

Later in the decades of the 1980s and 1990s, the term took on a slightly different connotation: the unspoken interpretation grew that a 'significant other' was a person's romantic lover, life partner, or in some way sharing a sexual and emotional connection (with no gender restriction). Armistead Maupin's book *Significant Others* (1987) brought wide and more accessible coverage to the term.

## 'Like a fish needs a bicycle'

*'(A) woman needs a man like a fish needs a bicycle' was the credo of Gloria Steinem.*

The image of the fish and the bicycle together originated over a decade before the word 'feminism' joined the language. American philosopher Charles S. Harris at Swarthmore College in 1958 observed in a college publication that 'A man without faith is like a fish without a bicycle.'

Some years later, across the Pacific Ocean, Australian author, editor and documentary film-maker Irina Dunn happened to read Harris's line. Being 'a bit of a smart-arse', as she later admitted to *Time*, she paraphrased the line into: 'A woman needs a man like a fish needs a bicycle.' In 1970 Irina Dunn boldly wrote the line inside two toilet doors — one at Sydney University, and the other in a Woolloomooloo wine bar. The expression spread widely and became a familiar part of the women's liberation movement.

It was often attributed to Gloria Steinem, but in 2000 Ms Steinem acknowledged that this was mis-attribution, by writing to *Time*, clarifying that Irina Dunn was the true progenitor.

# Mayday

*The distress call 'mayday' is English for the French term 'm'aidez'.*

Using the word 'mayday' dates from 1923, when a senior radio officer at Croydon airport was asked to think of an easily understood word which could be used to indicate distress. At the time there was considerable air traffic between Croydon and Paris, so radio officer Frederick Mockford invented the term 'mayday', supposedly based on the French *'venez m'aider'* (meaning 'come and help me') which he assessed that even in its abbreviated form would be understood by both French and British staff.

The term is widely understood — and when necessary used — in English, and in 1927 took some equality with the SOS distress signal (1908).

But there is a problem, because saying *'m'aidez'* would never occur at all in genuine French — it simply isn't correct. French people tend to call *'Aidez-moi'* (a polite request for help) or *'Au secours'* ('To the rescue'). However, the mangled 'mayday' has become established among English speakers, and in some circumstances French people will call SOS or sometimes 'mayday' — but using it as an 'English' expression.

# Snow

*The Eskimo language has 100 words for 'snow'.*

To begin, there is no such thing as one 'Eskimo language'. The term 'Eskimo' is used inaccurately to describe differing peoples from Alaska, Eastern Siberia, Greenland and Canada. Even using the more recently favoured term 'Inuit' doesn't cover the differences between the cold-region races. And within the cold Northern areas, at least half a dozen different languages can be heard, plus regional differences within those languages. So obviously the differing languages are likely to have differing words for common phenomena.

In 1911, anthropologist Franz Boas wrote *Handbook of the American Indian Language*, and made mention of some 'Eskimo' etymology: 'Here we find one word *apuvi* for snow on the ground. Another one *qana* — falling snow; a third *piqsirpoq* — drifting snow, and a fourth *qimuqsuq* — a snow drift ...' Unwittingly, Boas's simple paragraph (four lines in a scholarly and comprehensive tome about 'American Indians') kindled a folk myth which smouldered, then ignited into a slow fire whose flames kept burning for the next hundred years. The words 'which Eskimos have for snow' escalated into a belief way past the four Franz Boas originally mentioned.

Biological anthropologist Katherine Don explains that some languages from the Northern cold are 'polysynthetic', so that a word describing something can be attached to the word it's describing, making a compound coupling. Many descriptive words, such as 'heavy', 'light' and 'scattered', can be added to the basic word 'snow', giving the impression that there are many different words, although the basic word 'snow' has remained throughout and has been built on. Regarding each 'built-on' combination as a separate-entity word would give an almost limitless number of 'Eskimo' words for snow — so the perception grew that there were many separate words.

*The New York Times* once reputedly advised that there are 100. In 2013 *The Washington Post* narrowed it down to 40.

It can be perceived that a snow-prone countryside has many

ways of describing the differing ways in which snow affects daily life. If these 'differences' are attached to the basic word 'snow', it is perhaps over-defining to call that portmanteau word 'new'.

So scholarship remains in several different igloos about how many actual words the Northern cold places have.

English also perceives snow in various forms, but, except for 'snowman' and 'snowball', tends to keep the descriptor separate from the commodity it describes. Hence, we have only one basic word: 'snow'.

If by language evolution, the descriptor and the noun combined into one word (stranger things can happen) we too would have many words — by joining together 'snow' with: 'compact', 'powder', 'blizzard', 'flurry', 'hoar', 'slush', 'caps', 'storm', 'flakes', 'soufflé', 'blanket', 'mashed potato', 'drift', 'packed', 'sleet', 'storm', 'crust', 'whiteout', 'cauliflower', 'squall', 'avalanche', 'smud', 'melting', 'hardpack'. Then English would have 26 words for snow ... and ardent skiers could contribute several more.

## Condoms

*Condoms are named after King Charles II's physician, Dr Condom.*

It's a good story — pity it isn't true. In spite of widely distributed references to the philanthropic Dr Condom, to whom legend ascribes a royal-bestowed earldom, there is absolutely not a shred of evidence that there ever was such a person. Records of British aristocracy are meticulously preserved, and titles ancient and modern can be traced back 700 years and more. No such record exists for a Lord Condom (sometimes reported as 'Condon' — but that doesn't work either). And various forms of condom had been in use before Charles II's reign (1661–1685).

Even without 'His Lordship Dr Condom' there are various remaining possible explanations for the origin of the word 'condom', but not one of them has been proven satisfactorily. Nobody really knows how the word came into being. Except that it was not because of His Lordship Dr Condom.

# Marmalade

*Marmalade is a contraction of the term
'Marie malade'.*

The story goes that marmalade was served
to the French-speaking Mary Queen of Scots
when she wasn't feeling well, hence the name
'*Marie malade*'. Mary Queen of Scots lived in
France for nearly 20 years, and had been Queen
of France. But when she arrived back in Scotland in 1561, the
word 'marmalade' had already been in use in the English language
for nearly a hundred years. It came from the French word
*marmelade*, which in turn came from Portuguese, where *marmelo*
was the word for quinces, and quinces cooked with honey made
*marmelada* — a stiff quince paste.

The word's arrival in English was treated with some elasticity
— although originally the word 'marmalade' was recognised as
applying to sweetened quinces, gradually it became applied to
preserves made from almost any kind of fruit. As citrus fruits
slowly became more available, the name 'marmalade' shifted to a
large extent onto sweetened preserves made from oranges.

But it had nothing to do with Mary Queen of Scots feeling
poorly.

food and drink

## Tomato

*A tomato is a vegetable.*

It certainly is used that way. But the definition
of a fruit is: 'the ripened ovary of a flowering
plant containing one or more seeds'. Therefore
a tomato is formally classified as a fruit. Somewhat unwillingly,
we must therefore also include as fruits: peas, beans, cucumbers,
capsicums and pumpkins, which fulfil the same conditions.

Besides those mentioned, and others more recognised as fruits,
all the other parts of edible plants are vegetables: leaves (lettuce
and cabbage), buds (cauliflower and broccoli), stems (rhubarb
and celery), roots and tubers (beetroot, carrots and potatoes).

But apart from scientific definitions, a 'housewife's slogan' is
quite an effective way of allocating fruits and vegetables in the
practical sense:

If it goes well with ice cream — it's a fruit.
If it's good served with gravy — it's a vegetable.

## Apple pie

*'As American as apple pie.'*

Fondness for apple pies originated in Britain, where apples and
their pies had been popular for several hundred years before any

apples grew in America. In 1341 Chaucer gives a recipe for this attractive dish (intriguingly calling the pastry case a 'cofyn' — which was the usual terminology of the time). And a cookbook believed to have been compiled c.1390 by the master cook to King Richard II has instructions for making the classic apple pie. (Sir Edward Stafford later presented the book to Queen Elizabeth I.)

Apples suitable for pies didn't reach America until the seventeenth century, and another century went by before there were enough apples for commercial trade.

Commenting on the international success of Julie Andrews, a British guest on an American TV talk show once caused a frisson by describing her being 'as English as apple pie ...'.

## Mrs Beeton

*'First catch your hare' was
advice from Mrs Beeton.*

She didn't say it, or write it. There is no evidence that Mrs Beeton, Hannah Glasse, or any other famous cook, ever spoke or wrote this line, establishing the fairly obvious need to catch the main dish, before starting to prepare the meal.

The term was used by William Makepeace Thackeray in *Rose and Ring* (1855), but in a context not connected with cooking: rebel troops determined on usurping a Prince, track him to a tavern and demand his sword since he is the focal Royal. The Prince announces: 'First catch your hare. Ha!'

But whether it came earlier from anywhere else besides Thackeray is obscure to invisibility.

## Instant coffee

*Instant coffee was invented in Chicago in 1901.*

Perhaps they didn't notice that instant coffee had already been on sale for 11 years in the New Zealand city of Invercargill. Invented there by David Strang (patent no. 3518 in 1890), and described as 'soluble coffee powder — made instantly with boiling water — it can be made in a breakfast cup'.

Coffee mills in New Zealand had been established in Invercargill since 1872, and David Strang owned the Coffee and Spice Works factory, which produced spices, jellies, essences and coffee. Besides instant coffee, David Strang also pioneered another fashion: he mixed coffee with chocolate — later known as mocha.

## 'Shaken, not stirred'

*James Bond had a special cocktail.*

Only sometimes. Bond is depicted as being partial to a straightforward martini — either vodka or gin, famously 'shaken, not stirred' (*Dr No*, 1958). But true, there was a special cocktail invented by Bond in *Casino Royale* (1953): the 'Vesper' cocktail, named after the character Vesper Lynd.

Somewhat eccentrically, the 'Vesper' combines gin (three measures) with vodka (one measure), Kina Lillet (half a measure) and a shred of lemon peel ... and preferably the vodka used has been made from grain rather than potatoes. Ideally, the resultant mix was to be served in a deep champagne goblet.

The difficulty in re-creating an exact Bond 'Vesper' cocktail could be the availability of Kina Lillet. This is a blend of Bordeaux wines plus liqueurs derived from peels of Spanish and Moroccan sweet oranges, and the peels of bitter green oranges from Haiti, plus a derivative of Chinchona bark (containing quinine) from Peru. It is categorised as an 'aperitif', but clients less internationally mobile than Bond might have to use vermouth instead.

In recent years the Kina has been dropped from the name, and the mix is now known just as 'Lillet Blanc' – described by its makers as 'fresher, fruitier and less bitter'.

A martini being shaken not stirred long pre-dates Bond. It is an option mentioned in the *Bartender's Manual* by Harry Johnson (1882), and was then known as a 'Bradford' martini.

# Sandwiches

*Sandwiches were invented by the Earl of Sandwich.*

They weren't. The custom of putting a 'filling' between two firm edible slices had been in use for hundreds of years — as far back as the Jewish ceremony on the Eve of Passover when a mixture of apples and herbs is placed between two matzohs. Also, for several centuries cooked meats were placed on thick slices of bread (called 'trenchers') which soaked up the juices, and were then either eaten or thrown to the dogs. Placing another piece of bread on top of the food became a common practice in the sixteenth century, and was known simply as 'bread-and-meat' or 'bread-and-cheese.' Shakespeare mentions this.

*Larousse Gastronomique* (1961 edition) explains that:

> Since the most faraway time it has been the custom in the French countryside to give workers in the fields meat for meals enclosed between two pieces of wholemeal or black bread. Moreover, in all the south-west districts it was customary to provide people setting out on a journey with slices of meat, mostly pork or veal cooked in the pot, enclosed, sprinkled with their succulent juices, between two pieces of bread.
>
> Sandwiches made with sardines, tunny fish, anchovies, sliced chicken and even with flat omelettes were known in France well before the word, coming from England, had entered into French culinary terminology.

Enter Lord John Montagu, Earl of Sandwich. He joined the Admiralty in 1746 and became First Lord in 1748. He was also Secretary of State, former Postmaster General, sometime ambassador to Madrid, and with the rank of Colonel in the army (later appointed to General, though not in active service). He was a great supporter of Captain James Cook, and approved Admiralty funds for Cook to explore the Pacific. Cook named the Sandwich Islands after him (now Hawaii) and Montagu Island off Australia.

Lord Sandwich was very busy.

In 1765 a man called Pierre Jean Grosley wrote a travel book about London. In it he mentions an *unnamed* Minister of State who gambled with such absorption that 'he had no sustenance but a bit of beef between two slices of toasted bread, which he eat without ever quitting the game'. No name is mentioned, but centuries of over-confident conjecture have attached the description to Lord Sandwich — without the slightest evidence.

Lord Sandwich's later biographer, N.A.M. Rodger, explains that because of Lord Sandwich's demanding duties at the Admiralty, during the long hours he spent there both day and evening, meat-between-slices-of-bread *was* brought to the Earl, but at his *work desk*, not at gambling tables. (He particularly liked salt-corned beef.) That this became his recognised practice seems to have caused colleagues to order 'the same as Sandwich'. Hence the growth of the Earl's title being associated with the convenience snack — at least in the English language.

His penchant for portable bread-and-filling (and colleagues ordering 'the same as Sandwich') filtered through to other government officers and into general usage when it first appeared in print. Edward Gibbons wrote in 1762 of seeing more than 20 of the 'noblest and wealthiest' in a coffee bar 'supping on a bit of cold meat, or a Sandwich'. Just over a decade later, the word first appeared in an English cookbook (1773).

*Larousse Gastronomique*, the bastion of French culinary nomenclature, refers to 'sandwich' as 'a relatively recent name.'

Forget the nonsense about gambling.

Sandwich is a town in Kent, its locality recognised as far back as King Canute in 1028. There are many graceful and beautiful mediaeval buildings, and surviving gates from the ancient town walls. The name means 'sandy place on the mouth of a river'.

# Avocados

*Avocados are named from Spanish lawyers.*

It depends who you ask. The original fruit, when first observed by Spanish explorers in the Americas, had a name in the native Nahuatl language: āhuacatl, which means 'testicle', an uncompromising reference to the fruit's shape. From then on, a process called 'folk etymology' started to work on the Aztec word, to bring it into common usage without blushing — there was resistance to translating the fruit simply as 'testicle'. Spanish speakers turned āhuacatl into *aguacate*, which sounded similar to *abogado* — the Spanish word for 'lawyer' and the French *avocat*.

English speakers mis-heard these names, and they saw the rough-textured fruit's shape as being like a pear — thus leading to the corrupted version 'alligator pear', although the fruit has no relationship with alligators, pears or lawyers.

The University of California's Department of Agriculture and Natural Resources advises that the name we are familiar with — avocado — was first published by the distinguished naturalist Sir Hans Sloane in 1696. His catalogue of studied plants included: 'The Avocado or Alligator Pear-Tree. It grows in gardens and fields throughout Jamaica.'

The name 'avocado' which Sir Hans Sloane listed has been in use ever since. Easy to pronounce — and saving shoppers' sensitivity from having to ask whether the new season's testicles are in yet.

# Popeye and spinach

*Popeye ate spinach because its iron made him strong.*

It wasn't the iron. Popeye was created in 1929 by Elzie Segar. The rambunctious cartoon sailor had a spirited faith in spinach — his muscles could double in size after a meal of the crinkly green stuff. But why?

A folk-belief had grown that spinach contained large quantities of iron — which gave Popeye his strength. But criminologist Dr Mike Sutton of Nottingham Trent University points out that Popeye's creator, Elzie Segar, was not focusing on spinach because of its iron — *but because of its Vitamin A*. The first time Popeye mentions it is when he explains to Olive in a 1932 cartoon: 'Spinach is full of Vitamin A — an' thah's what makes hooman strong an' helty ...' In dozens of cartoons studied, Dr Sutton found that when Popeye slugged down spinach, it was *Vitamin A* keeping him 'helty'.

Among the many outings Popeye had in various media, were radio series in 1935, 1936 and 1937. The radio series was sponsored by breakfast cereal Wheatena, promoting how healthy it was. And ironically — you should pardon the pun — no references to spinach were allowed in the scripts.

## Sirloin

*Sirloin steak is so named because a king who enjoyed it named it 'Sir Loin'.*

Not at all. The word 'sirloin' describing a particular part of steak has been in English use since the 1400s. It is not derived from a king giving a knighthood, but from the French (as many English food words are: poultry, mutton, beef, pork, bully beef, sausage, venison, filet). In this case, old French *sur longe* meaning 'over the loin', which developed into *sur loigne* ... and, eventually, 'sirloin'.

## Sake

*Sake is a rice wine.*

It's not made from the juice of fruits, flowers or berries, so it can't (formally) be called a wine.

The alcohol in sake comes from sugars which have been

converted from the starch in rice. This fact — that it originates from grains — by definition makes it a beer (*Encyclopedia Britannica* defines sake as 'a rice beer'). Whisky is also derived from grain, but is distilled — which beer isn't. Sake resembles wine more closely than it does beer, so custom and usage tends to describe it as 'rice wine' although its alcohol content tends to be higher. Beer's alcohol can be up to 9 per cent, some wines can reach 16 per cent, but sake can get as high as 18 per cent alcohol (the level is sometimes deliberately reduced).

# Brazil nuts

*Brazil nuts must come from Brazil.*

Some do, but most come from Bolivia. And strictly speaking they're not nuts. Botanically, Brazil 'nuts' are classified as 'seeds'. Beside Brazil nuts being seeds, other 'botanically classified seeds' are: peanuts, almonds, pistachios, cashews, macadamia, pine nuts and coconuts(!). Real nuts include walnuts, chestnuts and hazelnuts.

# Brown eggs

*Brown eggs are more nutritious than white eggs.*

This is a nonsense. The colour of a hen's eggs can sometimes be predicted by the colour of her earlobes(!). In general, the darker the earlobes, the darker the eggs. Red, brown or black earlobes usually result in brown eggs, and hens with white earlobes usually provide white eggs. This is not a hard-and-fast rule; there are many exceptions. But it doesn't matter, because the nutritional value of the eggs, whether brown or white, is almost identical.

Perhaps there is some lingering earlier awareness of being told brown bread is healthier than white. But eggs aren't the same as bread. Both brown and white eggs contain approximately 70 calories per medium-sized egg, 210 milligrams of cholesterol,

12 grams of protein and up to 7 grams of fat. Both white and brown eggs are rich in B vitamins and in minerals such as phosphorus and choline.

So there is no appreciable difference between eggs whose shell is brown or white, either in nutrition or taste. Cook one of each and serve to someone blindfolded. They won't know which is which.

## Steak tartare

*Steak tartare was invented by the Tartars, while galloping their horses.*

'Steak tartare' is finely chopped or minced raw beef, mixed with either capers, chopped onions or shallots, salt, pepper, and sometimes Worcestershire sauce, and often served topped with a raw egg.

There is wide belief — now dismissed as a myth — that the name arose from a practice of Tartar warriors from the Volga region of Russia during the thirteenth century: habitually they would place slices of steak under their horses' saddles, so that at the end of a day's hard riding the steak would be tenderised and ready to eat.

*The Cambridge Mediaeval History* points to the fragment of fact behind the myth: namely, that sometimes Tartars *were* observed placing a small piece of meat under a saddle — not to eat, but where a horse had developed a sore, as it was believed that the fresh meat would help to heal it. The *History* then points out that

after a day's riding 'this meat, impregnated with the sweat of the horse and reeking intolerably, is absolutely uneatable'. (A much later variation on the myth — perhaps in a mood of American nationalism — attributed the meat-under-the-saddle story as being the province of early American cowboys.) So there is no place in the cuisine history of Tartary for 'steak tartar' (although in some later places and centuries, horse-meat has quite customarily been used as the meat therein).

But the development of what is known as 'sauce tartare' does have a connection, in that the Tartars are perceived (and chronicled) as a rough and tough race. So sometime during the early 1800s some unknown person developed a piquant if somewhat 'rough' sauce, which, theory has it, was named after the Tartars — because they, too, were rough!

'Tartare sauce' is a basic mayonnaise, mixed with (choose from): mustard; chives; chopped gherkins; tarragon; cucumber; parsley; vinegar; onion; chopped olives; lemon juice; horseradish; chopped boiled eggs. There is no single, finite recipe.

This sauce began to accompany the aforementioned serving of raw minced steak, known thereby as 'steak à *la tartare*'. Over time, the name of the additional sauce gravitated onto the meat itself, which became known as 'steak tartare' (sometimes 'tatare' or 'tartar').

## Humble pie

> To eat humble pie means to 'lower yourself — to be humble and apologise'.

The term 'humble pie' arose by mistake, and its origin has nothing to do with apologising.

In past centuries, there was — and still is — a perceived difference between eating the flesh of animals as opposed to eating the insides of animals. It wasn't uncommon for the grandees, the nobility, to be served venison, beef, mutton or pork, while the simple folk — the household servants and the huntsmen who'd brought home the animals — had to make do with the animals' discarded insides. And that which we know by the unattractive word 'offal' in earlier times was known as 'numbles'. Numbles were the kidneys, liver, heart, gizzard, etc., of animals — deer, sheep, pigs, and cattle — and were frequently made into a pie called a 'numble pie'.

By the 1400s the word 'numbles' had undergone a slight change and dropped its 'n', becoming 'umble'. But still the idea of eating offal — numbles — was somehow associated with people in a position of inferiority, and by the time 'numble' became 'umble' there began a mistaken association with the word 'humble' — meaning unpretentious and conscious of one's lowly position. There is no actual relationship between the word 'umbles' for offal and the word 'humble' for behaving apologetically: the internal organs — 'umbles' — are derived from the Latin *lumbellus* meaning 'a small amount of meat', and 'humble' comes from the Latin *humilis* meaning 'lowly'.

And as time went by, the perception of eating internal organs underwent a change, so that steak-and-kidney, or lamb's fry and bacon were not necessarily associated with people of lowly rank. But the confusion remained between (a) a pie made of 'umbles' and (b) a person required to get off their high horse ... they are described as 'eating humble pie'.

## Welsh rabbit

*'Welsh rabbit' should correctly be called 'Welsh rarebit'.*

No, it shouldn't. The delicious savoury dish made of melted (and sometimes grilled) cheese mixed variously with ale/mustard/paprika/Worcestershire sauce, and served on crisp toast, since at least the 1700s has been known by such various names as 'English rabbit', 'Irish rabbit', 'Scotch rabbit' ... and 'Welsh rabbit'. The Welsh appellation has survived better than the others. But in all cases the original recipes style the dish as 'rabbit'.

It is possible that the name might have arisen as a centuries-old ironic acknowledgment that people at that time not well enough off to afford butcher's meat, resorted to rabbits — if available. If not, the cheese became the protein *du jour*.

But even so, 'Welsh rabbit' comes into the perfectly respectable company of Bombay duck (which isn't duck), mock turtle (which isn't turtle), mock lobster (no lobster was damaged for this), and toad-in-the-hole (not necessary to be squeamish: there's no toad involved).

The famous cookbook of Hannah Glasse (1747) gives recipes for English, Scotch and Welsh rabbit. And *The British Housewife* by Martha Bradley (1755) gives Mrs Bradley's directions for Welsh rabbit. Neither lady mentions 'rarebit'.

It is possible that — any attempt at patronising aside — food mavens, including Escoffier, refer to the dish as 'rarebit' in order to clarify that it is vegetarian and contains no meat. But 'rabbit' is correct.

Since the early recipes from the eighteenth century, a development has occurred: Welsh rabbit served with a poached egg on top is called a 'Welsh buck rabbit'.

## Shrimp on the barbie

*Australians like to have 'another shrimp on the barbie'.*

A 1984 TV commercial featured actor Paul Hogan detailing with casual charm the attractions of Australia, on behalf of the Australian Tourism Bureau. His memorable final line was: 'I'll slip another shrimp on the barbie for ya.' But in fact Australians do not put shrimps on a barbie. The word 'shrimp' is never used in that country: when a shrimp or shrimps cross the Australian cuisine horizon they are always referred to as 'prawns'.

There is no scientific definition which differentiates between a 'shrimp' and a 'prawn'. The two words refer to exactly the same creature (Crustacea: Decapoda), but in different places.

In Australia the word 'prawn' is commonly used to describe what in America is called 'shrimp'. There is an informal concept that a shrimp is small and a prawn is bigger, but this is unsubstantiated, because both creatures can reach substantial size. At that point they are then referred to as 'king prawns' or 'jumbo shrimp' — depending where you are.

Australians do not need to have their own country advertised to them. Paul Hogan's catch-line about slipping a shrimp on the barbie was a deliberate use of the non-Australian word, because the commercial was aimed at an American market, which might have been confused at hearing the word 'prawn'.

Australians commenting on the commercial and its catch-phrase, tend to observe that they don't often cook prawns on a barbecue anyway — more likely 'snags' (sausages). But that might also have cause confusion to Americans, who tend to call sausages 'links'.

## Chutney and relish

*Chutneys are made with fruit, and relish with vegetables.*

Actually, they're basically the same.

'Relish' was originally a French word, used by the English since 1530 to describe 'a special enjoyment' — something available occasionally as a treat, even as nowadays you can 'relish' swimming in summer, or reading an enjoyable book, or a particular kind of movie. By the late 1600s, 'relish' had also come to mean something special and tasty added to the dinner table ... again, a little treat.

When the British started travelling to India a lot, they brought back spicy mixtures in jars from East India known by the Hindi word *chatni*. This was basically chopped-up fruits and vegetables treated with acids, sour herbs and hot flavourings. There were many variations in the ingredients: papayas, dates, raisins, mangoes, coconut, tomatoes, garlic, tamarind and onions. Plus vinegar, lemon juice, sugar, salt, coriander, mint and chillies.

Gradually, the new-fangled *chatnis* became the attractive thing added to the dinner table. And because they were something special, they qualified as a 'relish' to the meal — a little treat. Eventually the two words became interchangeable.

Some people insist that they are separate condiments: chutneys should be made with a fruit as the main ingredient (for example, mango chutney), and relishes are made with vegetables (for example, cucumber relish). But food experts concede that there really isn't a difference.

## 'Eat, drink and be merry'

> *The Bible tells us to 'Eat, drink and be merry for tomorrow we die'.*

The Bible doesn't say that. It's a combination of two separate lines in different parts of the Bible: 'Then I commended mirth, because a man hath no better thing under the sun, than to eat, and to drink, and to be merry' (Ecclesiastes 8:15) and 'Let us eat and drink; for tomorrow we shall die' (Isaiah 22:13). Neither line combines 'be merry' with 'tomorrow we die'. But a shortcut between the two, by custom and usage, has become a popular expression with a supposed 'biblical' origin — although it is actually a misquote.

## Oysters

> *Do not eat oysters in a month with no 'r'.*

This piece of 'advice' has a rather vague premise — and loses its point if you stop to think 'Which hemisphere does this apply to?'

The concept was first formulated by William Butler in 1599. His *Dyet's Dry Dinner* proclaims:

> It is unseasonable and unwholesome in all months that have not an R in their name to eat an oyster.

On close examination this appears to have no relevance to health or safety, but rather more with flavour and conservation. Northern Hemisphere oysters spawn during the warm months (May, June, July, August), and their texture and flavour is not as satisfying during this period. Also, leaving them alone during warm (and reproductive) months helps sustain the future oyster population.

But sophisticated techniques of farming and refrigeration have come a long way to overcome these matters, so in general *farmed* oysters worldwide can be available and eaten in all months of the year, although the pernickety prefer the supposed superior qualities of oysters 'from the wild'.

Therefore, Northern Hemisphere epicures who relish oysters brought in from the wild may still prefer to avoid them in months without an 'r'. But this does not apply in the Southern Hemisphere, where wild oysters spawn in the warm months — September, October, November, December — which have an 'r'; so conversely are best eaten in the winter months, which do *not* have an 'r' (May, June, July, August).

# Gin

*The name 'gin' comes from its origin in Geneva.*

Gin in its modern form has a long and complex history — none of it involving Geneva.

For centuries, many kinds of herbal infusions attempted to deal with various illnesses, using for example, sage, pennyroyal, willow bark, rosemary, lavender, valerian, ginko, dandelion, fennel, honeysuckle, ginger ... and juniper berries.

Franciscus Sylvius, a German-born medical scientist, became famous in the Netherlands as a professor of medicine, promoting ground-breaking research into the circulation of the blood, and the relationship between chemistry and digestion. And he is credited with creating, in 1650, a combination of grain alcohol with juniper berries (as a natural diuretic) for the treatment of gastric and kidney disorders. The mix was called *Jenever*, Dutch for 'juniper', from which the English word 'gin' is derived.

Juniper-flavoured alcohol became popular in the Netherlands, and was soon introduced to England by military men returning there from the Continent. When the Dutch King William of Orange became King of England, Scotland and Ireland in 1689, gin became extremely popular, and still is. But it is named after juniper berries — not Geneva.

## Carrots: raw or cooked?

*Carrots eaten raw are better for you than cooked.*

This is not necessarily correct. Carrots contain the desirable nutrient beta-carotene, but it is locked inside cells with high-fibre walls. When eaten in the raw state, the digestive system cannot deal with the high-fibre walls, and those cells pass through the body without releasing their nutrients into the system. But when cooked, the fibre is sufficiently broken down to make the beta-carotene readily available, and that nutrient becomes available to the body's system.

## Jerusalem artichokes

*Jerusalem artichokes must have originated in Israel.*

Alas no, they originated in North America, and have no connection with Israel or Jerusalem — and they aren't even artichokes.

Jerusalem artichokes can be found from eastern Canada down to Florida and Texas. They are a species of sunflower, with a tuber which is used as a vegetable. Native American Indians called the plant 'sun root', and the incoming pilgrims from England joined them in using the tubers as food. Other names — 'sunchoke', 'earth apple' — also came into use.

The current name has a haphazard history. Early settlers to America from Italy, noticing the resemblance of the sunchoke's flowers to the golden sunflower called it by the sunflower's Italian name — *girasole* ('turning towards the sun'). Then, whilst in America, French explorer Samuel de Champlain thought that the sunchoke tubers tasted like artichokes, and sent them to France and Italy — where again they were perceived as a sunflower. From there, English speakers heard *girasole* as 'Jerusalem', and de Champlain's assessment of artichoke flavour stuck, hence Jerusalem-plus-artichoke.

## Buffalo wings

*Buffalo wings must be chicken wings which are big!*

No, it's not the beast taking part in the title — it's the city. The recipe for these tasty snacks originated in the city of Buffalo in the state of New York. They are chicken wings which have been deep-fried, drained, then coated with a spicy sauce of melted butter containing vinegar and cayenne pepper. They are served still hot, with a cheese dressing and celery sticks.

## Pudding

*Pudding is the sweet dish served at the end of a meal.*

Not always. The English word 'pudding' is descended from ancient Continental words referring to things 'stumpy, thick or swollen'. It came to be associated with foods steamed or boiled inside some sort of bag or tube. Originally the term was applied only to savoury dishes, but has gradually moved towards dishes with sugar, fruit, rice and cream — particularly those which are boiled, baked or steamed, like Christmas pudding.

But the older terminology remains for some of the savoury dishes still to be found under their old names: Yorkshire pudding, black pudding (aka blood sausage), pease pudding and steak-and-kidney pudding.

# Hot cross buns

*Hot cross buns commemorate the death of Jesus.*

They do now, but in early centuries they represented other factors.

Many centuries before Jesus was born, buns in several civilisations were baked and marked with a cross, often believed to be associated with the moon. Some cultures held the moon as an influencing force (some still do — Christians commemorate Easter on a date dictated by the moon), so scholars believe that buns in ancient times were marked with a cross-shape on top, divided into four, representing the phases of the moon. And celebrations in early spring for the goddess Eastre (she whose name became the inspiration for the word 'Easter') coincided with a recognition of the contribution bullocks and oxen provided to the building of roads, dwellings and places of worship. On a special day to honour the beasts (which were also associated with the moon, who was seen to ride on the back of one), buns were baked with two pairs of bullock or oxen horns on top — one pair pointing up, the other, down — thus looking like a cross.

Whatever the ancient historic associations and reasons for shaping buns' tops into four, the later rise of Christianity saw the gradual taking over of long-existing festivals and symbols, and adapting them into the new religion. So the symbolic strength of oxen and the four phases of the moon were gradually assimilated into a new name 'hot cross buns', which, in spite of their new name, are seldom hot ...

# Kiwifruit

*Kiwifruit are native to New Zealand.*

They are in fact native to China. In 1904 a New Zealand school teacher noticed the plants when visiting the Yangtze Valley. They

were known in China by several colloquial
names including *yang-tao* ('monkey peach').
The teacher took seeds back to New Zealand, and
the plants flourished there, and New Zealanders called
their fruit 'Chinese gooseberries'. Commercial production
expanded, but a difficulty arose when exporting was
contemplated. Although known in New Zealand as 'Chinese
gooseberries' the fruit were not gooseberries, which
would confuse potential international markets (where the
fruit was virtually unknown). A suggestion of 'melon-ettes' was
discarded, because it transpired that melons had a high import tax
in some countries. So in 1959 the name 'kiwifruit' was invented,
and rapidly came into universal use.

A kiwi is an iconic native bird in New Zealand. But internationally
the word 'kiwi' has drifted into use as a single-word identification
for the New Zealand dollar, kiwifruit, the bird, or any New
Zealand person. Clarification is sometimes necessary, especially
if a New Zealander sees an American dessert menu offering 'ice
cream and kiwis'.

## Betty Crocker

*Betty Crocker was a well-known American expert on
home cooking.*

Alas, there was no Betty Crocker. She never existed. The image
of a friendly, knowledgeable housewife was imaginary, created
by the Washburn Crosby Company in Minneapolis in 1921, and
'she' was named after a retired director, William Crocker. The
company's women employees all provided a signature and the
'friendliest' one was chosen to finish off the replies to the letters
received by the company, asking for baking advice.

When 'Betty' advanced to radio in 1924 she was voiced by 13
different actresses, and somehow this invisible kitchen genius also
managed to write cookbooks.

In 1936 her first 'portrait' appeared, painted to look like an attractive 'composite' woman of no particular age. By 1949 'she' was on television, in the person of actress Adelaide Hawley Cumming, who played her for several years, and remained the 'living trademark' until 1964.

The painted 'portrait' of Betty often appeared in advertising, and was updated seven times — subtly acknowledging differing developments in fashion and kitchen activity, although growing mysteriously younger as the decades progressed.

A change in the marketing took place in 2006, and images of Betty became fewer, although the name remains as an icon of cooking knowledge.

# Brunch

*'Brunch' is a 'lifestyle concept' originating among upmarket Americans.*

 The word 'brunch' conjures an 'urban lifestyle' image of carefree Californians or glossy New York cafés, but both the word and what it describes, are British.

As far back as 1896, *Punch* reported that the word 'brunch' had been introduced the year before by British writer Guy Beringer:

By eliminating the need to get up early on Sunday, brunch would make life brighter for Saturday-night carousers. It would promote human happiness in other ways as well. Brunch is cheerful, sociable and inciting [*sic*].

So: a combined breakfast and lunch.

An afternoon version has evolved, characterised by culinary and alcoholic freedom, known as 'drunch'.

## Restaurateur

*A person who owns a restaurant is a 'restauranteur'.*

There's no 'n': the correct word is 'restaurateur'. The English word 'restaurant' comes from the French 'restaurer' — to restore, including restoring one's energy by eating. In French, 'ant' is equivalent to English 'ing', so 'restaurant' can be seen to mean 'a place of restoring'. The Latin ending 'ator' identifies that someone is acting out what the previous part of the word has specified, such as 'demonstrator', 'innovator', 'spectator'. Transferring into French, 'ator' becomes 'ateur.' So the person 'who is working at providing sustenance' is a 'restaurateur' — no 'n'.

## A chicken in every pot

*President Herbert Hoover promised American voters 'a chicken in every pot'.*

He didn't. One of his campaigners published that 'if Hoover were elected' there would be a chicken in every pot. However, Hoover never said the 'promise', although he is often misquoted as having done so.

There have also been muddled references to other US Presidents 'creating' the line. For example, FDR referred to it but never claimed to have created it, and JFK made a joking reference to it in 1960 when visiting Tennessee, where he implied that it hadn't happened.

However, the creator and only begetter of the original line was King Henry IV of France in 1589. A serious man, he supported agricultural development, arranged road-building, created more trade opportunities and encouraged prosperity for all citizens. His concern for the welfare of the general population helped him become one of France's most popular Kings. Historians report that his egalitarian attitude was summed up in his pronouncement in support of the working classes:

*Je veux qu'il n'y ait si pauvre paysan en mon royaume qu'il n'ait tous les dimanches sa poule au pot.*

I want that no peasant in my realm should be so poor that he not have a hen in his pot every Sunday.

King Henry's egalitarian wish became widely quoted beyond France, and in later centuries was appropriated by politicians elsewhere.

## Pineapples

*Pineapples are native to Hawaii.*

Pineapples are native to South America. They are known in many places as *anana* (which means 'delicious' in the area the fruit comes from). The first one believed to be raised in England was presented to King Charles II in 1661 (and he had his portrait painted with it).

But most people didn't realise that they grow down on the ground, not up in trees. In those times, the term 'pine-apple' was the generally used term to refer to what we now call 'pine cones'. Because this new fruit looked vaguely similar to a big cone on a pine tree, they too were called 'pine-apples', and it helped that their flesh was firm and sweet, like an apple.

Gradually, the term 'pineapple' moved onto the fruit permanently, and edged out its previous connection with pine trees, whose 'nuts' from 1669 onwards took on a new name: pine cone.

# i did it first

## Light bulb

*Thomas Edison invented the electric light bulb.*

Not quite. British physicist Joseph Swan demonstrated an electric light bulb in 1878 and patented it in 1880. Its current passed into and through a filament of carbonised paper. Swan's house was lit with these electric lamps, and in 1881 the Savoy Theatre in London became the first public building in the world lit with electric lamps — Swan's — and soon after Swan's electric lights began to illuminate Paris.

At the same time, Thomas Edison was working in America to improve the already existing versions of electric light bulbs available there. Edison also passed current through a filament, but of a slightly different type — and he, too, was granted a patent for that, also in 1880.

Edison continued working on modifying filaments, including filaments of carbonised bamboo, to improve the quality of light and the length of time the bulb would continue working. His improvements formed the basis for what is recognised as the modern electric light bulb. He gained recognition as the man who (eventually) created the basis for the type of practical electric bulb which became universally popular.

But apart from Joseph Swann, nine other inventors before Edison had ventured a version of an electric light. So Edison didn't invent it, but he improved an existing invention into practical use.

# Bloomers

*Amelia Bloomer invented bloomers.*

No. They were 'invented' by Elizabeth Smith Miller in 1851 — well, she adapted them for female wear. (Long baggy pants had been worn for years by both genders in Middle Eastern countries, and by Italian clowns.)

Amelia Bloomer was a well-known advocate of women's rights. She edited an early newspaper for women, and became well known as a spokesperson on social issues. When she was 33 she saw Elizabeth Miller's baggy pants (ankle-length, underneath a modest knee-length skirt) and immediately began to wear them. This caused much talk, and the baggies became known as 'The Bloomer costume'. Amelia wore them for eight years, then changed her mind, and went over to the crinoline. Although she wore this for the next 35 years, the impact she had made in Mrs Miller's 'bloomers' kept her name permanently attached to the garment and its future variations.

# Telephone

*Alexander Graham Bell invented the telephone.*

It's not clear. Bell gets the kudos, and Antonio Meucci is virtually forgotten.

Meucci, an Italian living in New York, demonstrated his version of a '*teletrofono*' in 1860, and set up the invention in his own home from basement to upper floors. But he lacked funds to pursue the formalities of commercialising the device and spreading its use. In December 1871 Antonio Meucci filed a 'patent caveat' for his '*teletrofono*' phone device. A 'patent caveat' was a description of an invention, lodged with the US Patent Office, notifying the *intention* of applying for a formal patent at a later date, but preventing the issue of a patent to anyone else with the same invention. This caveat did not require minute details of the proposed invention; it was less expensive that a 'real' patent;

and its legality lasted for 12 months, after which it had to be renewed. Antonio Meucci's finances didn't improve, and by 1874 he was living on 'public assistance' and was unable to renew his caveat on the proposed telephone invention.

An inventor called Elisha Gray was also working towards devising 'acoustic telegraph', and so was Alexander Graham Bell, a professional speech teacher. In 1876 both Gray and Bell filed patents with the US office — on exactly the same day! It has never been clear which was earlier than the other, but a belief that Bell copied Gray's submitted diagram was substantiated by a later sworn affidavit from a patent office examiner that he had shown Gray's diagram to Bell. In 1887 a court case was initiated by the US Government to annul Bell's patent on the grounds of fraud. Complications arising from changes in administration and the deaths of various key figures caused the case to be stymied in 1897 — leaving as 'undecided' the basic issue of who had actually *invented* the telephone: Meucci, Gray or Alexander Graham Bell.

As the survivor of the complexities, and the first to go commercial, with the Bell Telephone Company, the easy way out has always been to credit Alexander Graham Bell as the 'inventor' of the telephone. But to be accurate, after two earlier and acknowledged inventors, Bell *developed* the telephone towards the way it became successful.

## Guillotine

*The guillotine was invented in France.*

Not so. British historian Raphael Holinshed wrote in 1577 of there being versions of a guillotine used in Ireland since 1307. By 1400 England had its version — the Halifax Gibbet — and executions were held on market days. In Scotland, the National Museum of Antiquities in Edinburgh has an example dating from 1564, and known as 'The Scottish Maiden', and Italy was employing their version in 1702.

Over in France, in 1789 Dr Guillotin put forward his proposal to the Assembly Debate on Penal Code that death by decapitation should be the sole method of execution, and this was finally approved in 1791. The first French guillotining took place in 1792, and a year later the King of France, Louis XVI, was executed with the same machine. During the French Revolution, approximately 17,000 French aristocrats and 'enemies of the revolution' lost their lives by the guillotine. But not Dr Guillotin himself. He died in 1814 aged 76 — of a carbuncle.

# Tobacco

*Sir Walter Raleigh introduced tobacco to England.*

It would be safer to say Raleigh contributed to the popular use of tobacco in England. Jean Nicot had introduced tobacco into France during 1560–61, where it was found to help the royal migraines, and Queen Catherine de Medici dubbed it 'the Queen's herb'. (Nicotine was later named after Jean Nicot.)

At that time, sailors had more international experiences than most people in their homeland, including England. But sailors and their habits were below the notice of historical commentators, so occasional reports of English sailors with smoke coming from their nostrils were not accorded much attention. However, in 1564 when captain Sir John Hawkins (being socially placed somewhat higher than ordinary sailors) arrived back in England with his crew — and tobacco — it *was* noticed.

Sir Francis Drake evinced even more attention when he brought in a consignment of tobacco from the 'New World' in 1573. Twelve years later, Sir Francis Drake is believed to have introduced smoking to Sir Walter Raleigh. Raleigh was of course much higher on the English totem pole than John Hawkins (or any sailor in the street blowing smoke), and was able to mention it at the royal court and to the Queen.

So, while Sir John Hawkins attracted some notice at having introduced tobacco into England in 1564, it took another 20 years before Sir Walter Raleigh's association with the leaf brought it to wider attention, and helped popularise it — plus the occasional misbelief that he was the first to bring it to England.

## Molotov cocktail

*The 'Molotov cocktail' is a Russian invention.*

The Russian statesman Vyacheslav Mikhailovich Skryabin adopted the name 'Molotov' in 1906 in order to escape from the Imperial Police. (*Molotov* is Russian for a kind of hammer.) He was the Prime Minister of the Soviet Union from 1930 to 1941, and was Minister of Foreign Affairs during and after the Second World War. But he didn't invent the so-called 'Molotov cocktail', nor was it a Russian invention.

Early in 1940 Russia was fighting Finland, and it was the Finns who developed a homemade anti-tank bomb: a bottle filled with inflammable fluid and sealed, with a wick poking out the top. The wick was lit, then the bottle thrown at a tank. When it broke the liquid ignited and spread all over the tank plating.

This was widely adapted for use by the British Home Guard, and Mr Skryabin (aka 'Molotov') was intrigued with the device and organised the manufacture of similar devices in Russia. Thus the bomb became known by the Russian foreign affairs minister's nickname, 'Molotov'.

## Venetian blinds

*Venetian blinds originated in Venice.*

Maybe not. They were certainly known in Venice in early centuries, and were traded from there. But versions had been observed earlier in China, Egypt, Pompeii and Persia (Iran). Those earlier examples were simple in design, execution and materials, using reeds and bamboo. A legend that Marco Polo brought a gold-encrusted 'Persian blind' from Kublai Khan to Venice is difficult to substantiate.

But the traders of Venice had been expert since the Holy Roman Empire and before, so when they absorbed the concept of horizontal slat window coverings (from whatever source it came) they traded the design to the rest of Europe. France was using horizontal slat louvres and shutters in the 1600s — calling them *persiennes* — while in Italy they're called *persiana*. England had 'venetian blinds' in 1760, and America one year later.

## Iron Curtain

*Winston Churchill coined the term 'Iron Curtain'.*

Not at all. The term had been used many times before him. In literal terms, an iron curtain used to be a description of the fireproof panel which sealed off the stage in traditional theatres, preventing the possibility of any fire spreading from the stage to the rest of the theatre. But as a metaphor for 'a closing off', the term can be found in Arthur Machen's 1895 British novel, *The Three Imposters*: 'the door clanged behind me with the noise of thunder, and I felt that an iron curtain had fallen on the brief passage of my life'.

The first known use as a political image was in 1914 when German-born Queen Elisabeth of the Belgians referred to 'a bloody iron curtain' which had descended between her and her relatives in Germany.

It cropped up in Russian in 1918 when it appeared in *The Apocalypse of Our Times* by controversial Russian author Vasily Rozanov, translated as: 'With clanging, creaking, and squeaking, an iron curtain is lowering over Russian History.'

Ethel Snowden used 'iron curtain' in her book *Through Bolshevik Russia*, in 1920, and the famous Hungarian writer Ferenc Molnár used it in a 1927 play. Nazi propaganda minister

Joseph Goebbels used it several times; one occasion was reported in newspapers in February 1945.

As a political metaphor the expression has surfaced many times, from (among others) G.K. Chesterton, Sebastian Haffner and Douglas Reed.

Sir Winston Churchill was familiar with the term by at least 1945, when he used it in telegrams to the US President Truman, and then publicly in the House of Commons, August 1945: 'it is not impossible that tragedy on a prodigious scale is unfolding itself behind the iron curtain which at the moment divides Europe in twain'.

But sometimes an existing term is used in a circumstance which catches attention, and that person is afterwards credited with having invented the line. Sir Winston Churchill used the term 'Iron Curtain' in March 1946 during a speech in the United States to Westminster College in Missouri. In his speech (entitled 'Sinews of Peace'), he referred to the barrier of secrecy created by those Communist countries which had cut themselves off from Europe after the Second World War. The speech — and the line he used — became famous, and subsequently Churchill was often credited with having originated the term. He didn't — but he did make it famous.

## The Wright brothers

*The Wright brothers were the first men to fly.*

Perhaps not. There was also Gustave Whitehead. Who?

In March 2013, Paul Jackson, editor of the authoritative *Jane's All the World's Aircraft*, wrote that detailed research had made a reappraisal of the 'Wright Brothers were first' belief. He outlined the various circumstances of history (including the bombing of Jane's headquarters and destruction of records during the London Blitz), which had caused the achievements of Gustave Whitehead to have been treated to 'an injustice'.

In this honest reappraisal, Jackson reports that Whitehead invented a road-to-air 'flying car', and on 14 August 1901 drove in it for 15 miles to a Connecticut airfield, where he launched the vehicle into the air and flew. After coming down, he then launched it again and flew it a second time. All witnessed by the chief editor of the *Bridgeport Herald*. The ensuing published report of Whitehead's display triggered at least 85 other newspaper reports over the following year. By 1902, Whitehead had built a 40-horsepower diesel-fuelled craft for air transport only. He flew it on 17 January 1902 — confirmed by 17 affidavits from witnesses, and a 'recognising' technical article in the *Aeronautical World* publication of December 1902.

The Wright brothers have been credited with the 'first controlled, powered and sustained heavier-than-air human flight over a year later, on 17 December 1903'. And that reputation has been energetically maintained. The Smithsonian Institute's exhibit of the Wright's 'Flyer no. 1' was allowed by Orville Wright to be displayed, under a legal agreement that the Smithsonian would not state that any aircraft 'earlier than the Wright plane of 1903 ... was capable of carrying a man under its own power in controlled flight'.

The truth of this has been disputed by several other fliers, but the 'Wright legend' remained. Until now, when the impressive voice of *Jane's All the World's Aircraft* has approved and decreed that Gustave Whitehead was earlier.

Paul Jackson assesses that the Wrights' attitude to 'rigorous protection of their patents' and a careful avoidance of business partnerships with 'characters of unproven honesty' in the long run made their invention and their publicity more of a popular success. Jackson makes an analogy with 'the second mouse gets the cheese'. But in terms of who takes the ribbon for first place, Jackson concedes — 'Whitehead was ahead.'

# and god said

## Samson and Delilah

*When Delilah cut his hair, Samson lost his strength.*

She didn't do it. We are told little about Delilah except that she was a 'woman of Sorek'. (Soreq is a valley in the Judean mountains of Israel.) Bribed by Philistine lords to discover the secret of Samson's strength, she teased and upbraided him until 'his soul was vexed' and he confessed that his hair had never been cut and, if it were, his strength would be gone.

She then lulled him to sleep on her lap and called for 'a man', who came in and on her instruction shaved the head of Samson — who curiously remained asleep while being thus attended!

So a couple of movies, and all the many paintings, drawings and etchings showing Delilah wielding the scissors, have stretched the Bible way past what it actually recounts.

## Salome and the seven veils

*The story of Salome and her dance of the seven veils comes from the Bible.*

No, it doesn't. The name Salome and the image of a seven-veil dance do not appear anywhere in the Bible. Matthew (16:6) and

Mark (6:22) tell briefly about the young woman only as Herodias' daughter, but she is not named and there is no mention of veils or her style of dance.

In AD 94 the Roman-Jewish historian Flavius Josephus recounted the story, and in his version he claimed a name for her — Salome — and somehow an illusion grew that her name was mentioned in the Bible. It isn't, but the illusion has stuck.

Similarly there is an illusion that this biblical character danced, starting out with seven veils which were discarded one by one. There is not even the slightest hint of this in the gospel. But an ancient Babylonian legend (c.4500 BC) tells of the goddess Ishtar rescuing the soul of her dead husband by travelling to the underworld through its seven gates, and at each gate the price of admission was that she shed one of her seven cloaks or veils. So when she finally passed through the seventh gate, she was naked.

Eighteen hundred years after Josephus added a name to the brief Bible account of Herod's step-daughter, Oscar Wilde wrote his play *Salome* (1891, first performed 1896). Wilde apparently knew the centuries-old legend of Ishtar surrendering a veil at each of the seven gates to Hades. At the point in his play where Salome was to dance, Wilde wrote the stage direction: 'Salome dances the dance of the seven veils.'

Richard Strauss followed suit with the opera 'Salome' in 1905, and the 'Salome-plus-seven veils' fantasy was here to stay. But the Bible does not present the fantasy.

## Angels

*Biblical angels have halos and play harps.*

Various cultures have a place for spiritual creatures who could be identified as 'angels'. But painters and poets with romantic vision took lavish liberties when depicting angels within the Judaic-Christian tradition, completely circumventing the presumed authority — the Bible.

Angels are mentioned many times in the Bible: over 100 times in the Old Testament, and over 150 times in the New Testament.

But they are not female, at no point is there any mention of their having halos, and it is never said that they play harps. The only musical instruments associated with those heavenly angels are trumpets. Biblical references indicate that they are usually invisible, and are without gender, but can on occasion manifest themselves into visibility — usually male.

Only one ambiguous line (Zechariah 5:9) mentions a manifestation in female form, but it isn't clear that it refers to angels. The two women are not specifically called angels; indeed their wings are 'like the wings of a stork', which makes their being agents of God very unlikely, since storks are biblically 'unclean' birds. The two women are not regarded as evidence that angels are female. Wings get scarce mention elsewhere, since it is fairly clear that biblical angels can travel anywhere without aid, but Isaiah does mention 'seraphim' with six wings: two covering their faces, two covering their feet, and the other two for flying.

Harps figure rarely in the scriptures — and never with angels. Revelation 14:2 tells of: 'a voice from heaven, as the voice of many waters, and as the voice of a great thunder: and I heard the voice of harpers harping with their harps'. But nowhere does it say that angels are playing them.

Be careful of seraphim, too. Ezekiel says:

And every one had four faces: the first face was the face of a cherub, and the second face was the face of a man, and the third the face of a lion, and the fourth the face of an eagle.

## Three Kings

*Baby Jesus was visited by three kings.*

The Bible never mentions kings visiting Jesus, nor how many. The 'wise men' who visited the baby are not given any royal rank, nor is the number of them mentioned. Perhaps the giving of three gifts

— gold, frankincense and myrrh — gave rise to an impression that there were three people, even though this isn't specified.

Myrrh is the sap of a thorny *Commiphora* shrub. In ancient times it was very expensive, and was used for embalming dead bodies, and also being burnt at funerals to disguise the smell of bodies which hadn't been embalmed. In modern times, it is very good for healing ulcers in the mouth. It is difficult to understand why myrrh was given as a present to a young child!

## Adam and Eve

*Adam and Eve ate a forbidden apple.*

We don't know; the Bible doesn't say. It just says a 'fruit'. That it was an apple is a mysterious assumption which has crept into common use. There is speculation that confusion may have existed in translation (into English), but there is no real evidence or reason for this.

Other candidates which have been speculated instead of an apple include a fig, a grape, a date, a pomegranate or a pear. There's no evidence about them either.

# Methuselah

*Methuselah lived to be 969 years old.*

Apart from those parts of the Bible which have been mis-heard or somehow attached to something which isn't actually there (see 'Salome', 'Three Kings', etc.), the Bible does clearly say that Methuselah sired children when he was 182 years old, then lived on to the age of 969 (Genesis 5:26).

It is quite difficult to accept this as fact, within the fabric of faith which the Bible engenders. There have been some defences put forward against the seeming impossibilities:

➡ That in antediluvian times, before mankind saturated the atmosphere with radiation and global warming, people in such pure air could actually live that long.

➡ That the lifestyle of the human race has brought about a gradual degeneration in heath, and people are dying much younger (than 600) now.

The use of the word 'years' is a misconcept, and could mean 'lunar months'. (This strikes a wobble when you start dividing, since it would mean that Abraham lived only around 14 years, if his 175 represents lunar months. And Isaac, who supposedly sired his sons at 60, would in lunar months have been only five years old.)

But historical writer Robert M. Best is convinced that the confusion lies in translation from the original texts. He explains that the sources of Genesis can be found in three different ancient languages: Masoretic, Samaratin and Septuagint. He contends that the long-ago compiler of the Genesis we know re-calculated the numbers from the ancient text he was using (thought to be from 2600 BC) into a number system familiar at the time — in which time was calculated in years and tenths of years (presumably their version of a 'month'). He could have used: 'One or more archaic number signs for *tens*, a different sign for *units*, and a different sign for *tenths*.' Hundreds of years later in the Old Babylon period

(1800 BC) a scribe re-translated the numbers in the 'cuneiform' system then in practice. Carefully tracking this ancient system and comparing it through various earlier translations and historic calculation methods into the Genesis we know, Robert Best calculates that the truth lies somewhere in our calculating: 'tens of years into *hundreds*, years into *tens of years*, and tenths of years into *years*.'

According to Robert Best's very practical-seeming calculation, this explains that Methuselah's death aged 969 actually happened when (in our arithmetic) he was aged 96 years 7 months. We might never know, but Best's interpretation at least gives the comfort of possibility.

## Jesus' birthday

*Jesus was born on 25 December.*

Nobody knows when he was born. But a centuries-old festival was held during the coldest month, celebrating the turning point of the Northern Hemisphere winter towards spring. Three hundred years after Jesus' (guessed-at) death date, Pope Julius I announced that the solstice festival, now settled on 25 December, would *also* be the date to 'celebrate' Jesus' birth. As Christianity grew in numbers, 25 December seamlessly overtook the existing festivities and gradually became 'Christmas'.

## Noah's flood

*Noah and his ark were adrift for 40 days and 40 nights.*

More. They were *rained on* for 40 days and 40 nights, but the flood caused by the rains lasted much longer. Genesis 8:3 tells that the rain and its following flood together totalled 150 days.

# Catholics and divorce

*Catholics are not able to divorce.*

Yes, they are. Starting in the sixteenth century, many countries started moving the two matters of marriage and divorce into the nations' legal systems. Some organised faiths had taken it upon themselves to decree that those who chose to follow that faith must abide by a faith-imposed decree that a marriage may not be dissolved. But gradually this was worn away — and once placed within the legal system, any other 'rules' from outside organisations have no strength in law.

In a country where law governs marriage and divorce, no church has any authority over either of those. Only those people with a personal wish to follow a faith-imposed restriction may elect to deny themselves what the law actually does allow. A couple who provide satisfactory evidence to the State and have followed its legal procedure, can be lawfully married. Also, should serious friction later occur, the State has a system whereby a legal marriage can be undone, and a legal divorce is declared. Nobody else has any control over these.

In *Untying the Knot*, his study of divorce history, Professor Roderick Phillips of Carleton University, Ontario lists the transition of divorce into a status of law, even if censured and denied by 'decrees' from a faith. The move began in Europe, spurred by Martin Luther's rejection of religious control over private unions. Examples grew: Switzerland established legal divorce in 1533, Scotland in 1563, Denmark, Norway and Iceland in the 1580s.

Divorce in America was first established as a matter for a court of law in 1643, with the divorce of Anne Clarke, in the Quarter Court of Boston, Massachusetts. The later United States' Constitution made no decree about divorce, and over the following century the separate states developed their own divorce laws, and jurisdiction by each state remains; there is no federal jurisdiction over their divorce rulings.

England was surprisingly slow. By various bits of juggling over the centuries, men were sometimes allowed to instigate divorce but women weren't. The matter eased out in 1857 with England's Divorce and Matrimonial Causes Act, which moved divorce into general application (women or men could apply) and under decision according to law only, distanced from any ecclesiastical pronouncements.

# the animal kingdom

## St Bernard dogs

*St Bernard dogs rescued travellers in the snow, carrying little brandy barrels.*

Forget the little brandy barrels — this is a legend which turns out to be a myth. St Bernard dogs could anticipate an avalanche before it began, and could locate people buried under 3 metres of snow. But they never carried little barrels of brandy. This image was totally invented by English painter Edwin Landseer, who in 1831 painted *Alpine Mastiffs Reanimating a Distressed Traveller.* The painting showed one of the St Bernard rescue dogs with a little barrel on its collar — a barrel which came out of Landseer's imagination — as did his explanation that the little barrel 'contained brandy'. And a legend was born.

People were inspired to believe that this was the norm, and the 'brandy barrel' image became part of popular belief for generations. Shops selling 'dog accessories' quickly made 'St Bernard collars' available (with miniature barrel attached), and the image became almost permanent. But it was never based on fact. The dogs just didn't carry brandy!

# Crocodile tears

*Crocodiles sometimes weep tears.*

Crocodiles can't cry. Apparently there is some basis for the belief that occasionally small drops of fluid are exuded from crocodiles' eyes — possibly to aid their chewing as they trickle down, or possibly activated by the movement of their jaws, or the heat of the sun. But whatever the cause, it is a physical reaction not an emotional one.

These 'tears' may have caused the belief that crocodiles weep as they demolish their victims, which is mentioned in ancient Greek and Latin texts. The thought was first seen in English when Sir John Maundeville's book *Voyage and Travail* appeared in 1400. Sir John wrote: 'There be great plenty of Cokadrilles — These serpents slay men, and then weeping, eat them.' The image of emotion falsely displayed, based on Maundeville's crocodiles being sorrowful over their lunch, has been with us ever since.

# Elephants

*Elephants never forget.*

Elephants can remember jungle pathways, the location of burial grounds, family members, other elephants they have met, and learned commands given by howdah drivers. In other words, their memories are similar to — and not noticeably bigger than — those of many other animals. The idea that the elephants are good at remembering simply everything has little basis. It seems to have arisen from a line from British writer H.H. Munro ('Saki'), born in Myanmar and a former member of the Burmese police, and thus very familiar with elephants. In 1904, one line in Saki's story 'Reginald on Besetting Sins' introduced English readers to the concept of elephants having good memories: 'Women and elephants never forget an injury.' But even he doesn't proclaim exactly by what boundaries the elephant's memory abides.

So we accept that, efficient though they are, there is no evidence that an elephant's memory is ... elephantine.

# Hippopotamus

*The hippopotamus is a water animal.*

Yes, it is. The word *hippo-potamus* is derived from two Greek words meaning 'horse of the water'. But, curiously, although a horse can swim, a hippopotamus can't.

# Noah's ark

*All the animals entered Noah's ark two by two.*

Two — or seven? It's not that simple.

At one point the Bible reports that Noah is instructed to take 'two of every kind', but elsewhere the report says: 'Of very clean beast thou shalt take to thee by sevens, the male and his female, and of beasts that are not clean, by two, the male and his female. Of fowls also of the air by sevens.' So the clean beasts and the birds — in sevens — would have been three pairs, plus one left over (perhaps should one of the seven become inoperative). And the 'not clean' beasts were in the legendary two-by-two.

'Arkeologists', who believe the report to be literal, must worry about dinosaurs and brachiosaurs presuming they existed then, as they would take up an enormous amount of room, whether in twos or sevens. But then the mosquitoes didn't need much room at all ...

# Greyfriars Bobby

*Greyfriars Bobby was a terrier who sat by his
dead master's grave for 14 years.*

Maybe not. The legend tells that Bobby, a Skye terrier, was the inseparable companion of an Edinburgh night-watchman, John Gray, who died in 1858 and was buried in Greyfriars Kirkyard. For the next 14 years his dog, Bobby, wandered the graveyard and every day sat on the grave, waiting for his master, who (obviously) never returned. Bobby's devotion became famous — he was given a licence by the Lord Provost of Edinburgh, with a special collar inscribed *Greyfriars Bobby from the Lord Provost*. The collar is now in the Edinburgh Museum.

Bobby died in 1872, and Baroness Burdett-Coutts arranged the installation of a granite stand with a statue of Bobby on top. Its inscription reads:

Greyfriars Bobby
Died 14th January 1872
Aged 16 years
Let his loyalty and devotion be a lesson to us all.

Bobby's story has been told in books, television, songs and several movies, and many tourists have visited the place of his activities.

But the legend may not be true. Dr Jan Bondeson of Cardiff University felt some doubts, and applied diligent research to the story. His conclusion was firm: Greyfriars Bobby was partly a hoax and an illusion! There is no actual evidence of who Bobby's deceased 'master' was, or whether the dog had ever been attached to anyone buried there.

Furthermore, Dr Bondeson studied available likenesses of Bobby during his 14 years' graveside devotion, and concluded that two different dogs were involved. By appearance, age, and even a change of breed, he ascertained that the 'original' Bobby had probably died in 1867. But by then the legend was established, and it was 'good for local business' that tourists kept coming, so a replacement was hastily found (Dr Bondeson's study of comparative illustrations revealed a younger dog of a different breed) and was taught the graveyard routine. But researched proof or not, Dr Bondeson acknowledges that perhaps the public prefers the legend to the truth.

## Peacocks' tails

*Peacocks have spectacular and beautifully coloured tails.*

Actually the peacock's tail feathers have very little colour at all, save for a dullish pale brown. The colours of some birds rely on pigments within their feathers' structure — but the peacock has no pigments. What it does have is 'structural colouration'. Each peacock quill has many feathery strands branching off it, and each strand is made up of tiny filaments called 'barbules'. These have a microscopically structured surface which 'interferes' with visible light and can reflect it back in differing wavelengths, thus in differing colours. So, in the case of the peacock, the incoming light reflects back to the viewer's eye as superbly organised complex patterns in green, yellow, brown and blue. From some angles, the 'colour' being 'scattered' into the viewer's eye is also accompanied by a shimmering non-colour overlay of iridescence. (The underside of a CD or DVD can sometimes demonstrate a smaller but similar phenomenon of 'structural colouration' plus 'iridescence' from a basically non-coloured surface.)

This extraordinary visual illusion of the peacock tail has been known since at least 1665, when member of the Royal Society (and curator of its experiments) Robert Hooke studied peacock feathers and wrote in his book *Micrographia*:

> The stem or quill of each Feather in the tail sends out multitudes of Lateral branches, ... so each of those threads in the Microscope

appears a large long body, consisting of a multitude of bright reflecting parts.

Their upper sides seem to consist of a multitude of thin plated bodies, which are exceeding thin, and lie very close together, and thereby, like mother of Pearl shells, do not only reflect a very brisk light, but tinge that light in a most curious manner; and by means of various positions, in respect of the light, they reflect back now one colour, and then another, and those most vividly.

Mr Hooke also observed that a similar method of 'scattering' received light to send it back as multi-coloured is found in kingfishers and some butterflies.

## Bumble-bees

*Scientists say that, theoretically, bumble-bees shouldn't be able to fly.*

Well ... one scientist did.

In 1934, French entomologist Antoine Magnan studied the proportion between body weight and wing capacity of insects — including the wings' size and beats per second. In 1934, in his book *Le Vol des Insectes* (*The Flight of Insects*), he published his conclusion:

First prompted by the fact of aviation, I have applied the laws of the resistance of air to insects, and I arrived at the conclusion that their flight is impossible.

Note that he was writing about the flight of *all* insects. For no coherent reason, that one line somehow crept out of a moderate scientific treatise, in a narrowed version. It then became modified, and blossomed into folklore as: 'according to scientific principles, bumble-bees should not be able to fly'.

This was certainly not true, but became a widespread urban legend. Apart from the obvious fact that bumble-bees knew nothing about this, and happily continued flying, scientists disproved the thesis, and eventually Magnan himself retracted. But the misbelief has staying power and has not entirely died out.

## Goose-step

*The Nazi 'goose-step' has that name because it resembles geese walking.*

Real geese walking bear no resemblance to the stiff-legged military march which has that name. Stiff-legged 'goose-stepping' in the military context was first introduced in Prussia, by Fieldmarshall Prince Leopold of Anhalt-Dessau (1676–1747) and was never called anything to do with geese. In the German language the existing phrase 'goose march' (*Gänsemarsch*) referred to children walking in single file behind a parent, as goslings do. The Prussian military leg-high march was known as *Stechschritt* — the 'piercing step.'

The expression 'goose-step' was in English use as early as 1849 when a *Punch* cartoon showed English military recruits learning an exercise which in no way resembled the rapid stiff-legged gait later associated with goose-stepping. But there was also a military gait known as 'slow march': bearing the weight on one foot and suspending the other outstretched leg until the command was given to lower the weight onto the projecting leg, and repeat the routine with the other leg — *ad infinitum*. Standing immobile on one leg for a time was faintly reminiscent of how a goose often stands, and both the exercise and the resulting slow march looked slightly ridiculous. Thus, looking 'as silly as a goose' and the nickname 'goose-step' aligned itself with the stiff-legged 'slow march' sometimes seen in Britain at that time. The word 'goose' has carried a pejorative sense in English since the sixteenth century, as in 'you silly goose'.

The concept of looking 'as silly as a goose' appears to have been transferred from the quite sedate British slow march, to poke fun at the high-step ceremonial German march, which became infamous during the twentieth century.

The end of the Second World War did not end the practice of 'goose-stepping'; many nations throughout the world still use some form of it as part of formal military parading.

## Dick Whittington's cat

*Dick Whittington's pet cat was an excellent ratter and helped make Dick's fortune.*

Dick Whittington was a real person and he really was Mayor of London three times (1397–99, 1406–07 and 1419–20). But he was not from a poor family (his father was Sir William Whittington), and there is no evidence whatever that he at any time owned a cat. The only connection he is known to have had with a 'cat' was in connection with his trade (velvets and expensive fabrics for aristocrats) and their being conveyed up and down the Thames in 'cat-boats'.

He died in 1423, and, over 180 years later, fanciful tales about him began to emerge — first published in 1605. Further colourful additions to the slim basic historical facts continued to become part of folklore, and in 1814 came the ultimate fanciful version: a London pantomime, starring the famous Grimaldi as the Dame Cecily Suet, a cook.

The 'additions' to the story included his leaving London and being told by a mystery voice to return — as mayor. A statue of him in full London mayoral robes stands outside the Royal Exchange in London.

And even if Dick Whittington had a 'cat-boat' rather than an actual cat, the legend is powerful enough for the Establishment to recognise its charm — so a memorial statue of 'Dick Whittington's cat' can be seen crouching on a plinth at the foot of Highgate Hill in North London, where reputedly Dick heard the bells of Bow church tell him to return to London where he would three times be mayor.

## Turkeys

*Turkeys are so called because they originated in Turkey.*

Turkeys are virtually unknown in Turkey. The birds are believed to have originated in what we now call Mexico. Before turkeys were ever seen in England, an earlier bird which came from Africa had been brought to Continental Europe, and was gradually spread further by busy international traders, many of whom hailed from the Eastern edge of Europe, and were colloquially known as 'Turkish merchants'. Because of them, this exotic-looking bird was casually named a 'turkey fowl.'

But a hundred years later, another exotic bird was brought to notice in England, and confusion arose because of the way it looked — because it seemed remotely possible it could be a relative of the 'turkey fowl'. So it, too, became known as a 'turkey'. Obviously this was confusing, and it took a while to sort out. But eventually the first of the exotic-looking birds was re-named after the area where they'd been brought from — the part of Africa known as the Guinea Coast. So those birds became 'guinea fowl'.

And when the guinea fowl relinquished a connection to Turkey (a connection which they didn't rightly have anyway), the other larger Mexican bird retained the name of that same nation — a nation with which it had even less connection. But in English it is still known as a 'turkey'.

Guinea fowl originate from the Guinea Coast of Africa, but 'guinea pigs' don't — they come from South America.

# Nightingales

*The poet John Keats heard a nightingale sing and wrote the famous poem 'Ode to a Nightingale'.*

It's a lovely thought, and a famous poem ... but Keats made a mistake: he refers to the nightingale as a 'light-winged dryad of the trees' who 'singest of summer in full-throated ease'. Dryads are beautiful creatures in Greek mythology. They are spirits of the trees and they are always female. But female nightingales don't sing — only males do.

The imagery becomes more confused with the writings of Keats's friend, Charles Armitage Brown, who reported that the bird we are being told about had built its nest near his (Brown's) home in 1819, and that Keats felt a 'tranquil and continual joy in *her* song; and one morning he took his chair from the breakfast table to the grass plot under a plum tree, where he sat for two or three hours'.

If it was a lady nightingale, there would have been nothing to hear. Poetic licence transformed a male bird (which presumably is what Keats *did* hear) into a female 'dryad'.

He wasn't the only one. Shakespeare makes the same mistake — Juliet tells Romeo:

Believe me, love, it was the nightingale.
Nightly she sings on yon pomegranate tree.

No, 'she' doesn't.

# Polar bears

*Polar bears are white.*

Polar bears certainly give that impression. They look white — but they are not, their hide is actually black. The hide is covered with

a dense undercoat and an impressive top coat, which is made up of hairs which are completely transparent. Each hair is hollow and has no pigment. From the hundreds of separate hairs, the hollow spaces inside scatter all of the light which reaches there. This results in the effect of white, because the colour white registers to the eye when an object reflects all the visible wavelengths (rather than absorbing them).

The US Fish and Wildlife Service confirms that when the bear is seen in sunlight, the sun's rays bouncing back from the hollow core of hundreds of transparent colourless hairs make the polar bear's coat *appear* white. But behind all the colourless white-seeming fur lies a black skin!

## Chameleon

*Chameleons can change colour depending on their surroundings.*

They can change colour, but not because of the colour of their surroundings.

There are over a hundred species of chameleons: lizard-like creatures up to 25 centimetres long, primarily tree-dwelling, with bulging eyes which can move independently and often with head 'ornamentation'.

They do have a remarkable ability to change colour: many of their cells contain granules of pigment which are controlled by the nervous system. Differing species have access to a diverse range, including green, yellow, cream, brown, pink, blue, orange, green and black — with patches of one colour superimposed on another.

But it is a misconception that the colour changes are always dictated by a wish to 'blend' with the surroundings. The smaller, more vulnerable chameleons can sometimes camouflage them-selves temporarily, but only when threatened by a predator. In general, the chameleon's body colour changes according to factors such as temperature, fear, victory, defeat, levels of light — and courting behaviour.

# Lemmings

*Lemmings commit watery suicide when the numbers need reducing.*

Lemmings are small furry rodents which live in the Arctic Circle area. They do not engage in mass suicidal dives off cliffs, or march into the sea when migrating. Sometimes, when venturing into unknown territory, the odd animal has accidentally fallen and occasionally has been found drowned. The uncommon sighting of a drowned lemming became the germ of a growing myth that death was a deliberate act on the part of the deceased lemming — but this is not so.

The myth was sustained and publicised in the 1958 Disney film *White Wilderness*, which showed scenes of lemmings 'migrating' and 'committing suicide'. The lemmings in the film had been imported from their normal habitat into the city of Calgary. The filmed scenes of them 'migrating' were falsely staged using multiple shots of different groups of lemmings on a large, snow-covered turntable in a studio. The lemmings were later pushed off a cliff, and photographers placed below filmed them actually just falling — but supposedly jumping into the water.

In real life lemmings don't do that.

# Cleopatra and the asp

*Cleopatra died by allowing an asp to bite her.*

We'll never know if that was what happened.

She died in 30 BC and no first-hand report exists of how her death happened: all so-called 'accounts' are speculative. They agree that only two of her personal servants were with her when death came. But from what cause, or by what means, proven history is silent. Nobody has ever known. She was 39.

One hundred and thirty years after she died, Roman scholar Plutarch put down a description about her method of death, which has gone into popular belief:

> Some relate that an asp was brought in amongst those figs and covered with the leaves, and that Cleopatra had arranged that it might settle on her before she knew, but, when she took away some of the figs and saw it, she said, 'So here it is,' and held out her bare arm to be bitten.
>
> Others say that it was kept in a vase, and that she vexed and pricked it with a golden spindle till it seized her arm.
>
> But what really took place is known to no one.
>
> Since it was also said that she carried poison in a hollow bodkin, about which she wound her hair; yet there was not so much as a spot found, or any symptom of poison upon her body, nor was the asp seen within the monument; only something like the trail of it was said to have been noticed on the sand by the sea, on the part towards which the building faced and where the windows were. Some relate that two faint puncture-marks were found on Cleopatra's arm.

The ominous words 'Some relate' and 'it was also said' indicate that Plutarch was relying on hundred-year-old hearsay, not direct evidence. Other writers have proposed different theories through the centuries.

Thomas North's 1579 translation of Plutarch's *Lives* is credited with being the inspiration for Shakespeare's *Antony and Cleopatra*, a very cogent promoter of the 'bitten by a snake' death.

The word 'asp' is a worry. There is a kind of snake called an asp, but at this distance in time and many translations, 'asp' could possibly mean just 'snake'. But what kind? Small enough to fit in a basket of figs, yet potent enough to kill three people very quickly. 'Asp' can refer to an Egyptian cobra, which is very poisonous.

But contemporary cultural historian Lucy Hughes-Hallett (1991) has made a close study of everything known (and speculated) about Cleopatra, including the 'snake' story. Her detailed study of the various scenarios results in the view that: 'To have secreted enough venom to have killed her and her two women, the cobra would need to have been about six foot long.' Which rather destroys the 'bowl of figs' image.

Perhaps the most salient line of Plutarch's is: 'But what really took place is known to no one.'

## Camels

*Camels can go without drinking because they store*
*water in their 'hump'.*

There is no water in the camel's hump — it contains fatty tissue, from which their system gains sustenance when conditions get difficult.

Various features of the camel's build and metabolism give it the ability to go without drinking for some time. When the camel exhales, water vapour becomes trapped in its nostrils and is reabsorbed into the body as a means to conserve moisture. Its body temperature can rise considerably during the day, thus avoiding losing too much moisture by sweating. The thick coat is an aid to desert survival — when sweating does occur it evaporates at the level of their skin, rather than on the outside level of their coat. In extreme temperatures, a camel can survive losing up to a quarter of its body weight by sweating — more than twice any other animal could withstand and still survive. When water becomes available, they can restore their body weight quite soon, with an extraordinary capacity for drinking large quantities: 25 gallons (94 litres) or more.

The fatty deposits in the hump are also a help. When needed, fatty tissue is drawn into their system and releases energy which helps conserve moisture. But there is no actual water in the hump.

# Santa's reindeer

*Santa's eight reindeer must be very strong to carry him around the world!*

Indeed they must be strong — particularly as they're all female!

Santa is invariably depicted with eight athletic reindeer powering through the winter air, all sporting spectacular and elegant antlers. But The Alaska Department of Fish and Game points out that male reindeer lose their antlers in winter and females retain theirs ... so those associated with Santa's image must be ladies. There is one other possibility: some male reindeer retain their winter antlers if they've been castrated, and castrated reindeer are known to grow somewhat bigger and stronger than their unmolested brothers. So with that exhausting night ahead of him, maybe Santa has chosen ... but no, that thought somehow doesn't meld well with what we want to hear.

# Centipedes

*Centipedes have 100 legs.*

Not always. 'Centipede' does mean '100 legs', but it is not a formal scientific description, just an informal popular way of referring to a particular group of skinny arthropods, which have many legs.

How many? The centipedes' long bodies are in segments — always an uneven number of segments, and each segment has a pair of legs. The number of legs varies enormously among the (several thousand) different species. Some have only 30 legs, while others have well *over* 100.

# Swans

*Swans sing only once — just before they die.*

Swans utter a variety of sounds. Across different species, their output is described as: trumpeting, whistling, grunting, snorting, whooping, hissing or honking. But not singing. Not even when they are dying.

The myth about them singing before death descends from the mythology of Ancient Greece, which often involved swans. Helen of Troy (if she existed at all) was born of an intimate union between Queen Leda of Sparta and Zeus, who had changed himself into a swan for taking part in that intimate union. The notion that dying swans sing dates back to at least 458 BC, mentioned by Aeschylus in one of his 90 hit plays of the time. (It is to Aeschylus we owe the invention of stage 'dialogue' between characters, hitherto unknown.) Later, Plato reported Socrates as believing that swans sang beautifully before they died, and Aristotle agreed.

So the fable came with good references — but fable it is. Swans do not sing at any time during their life, and not before they die.

Pliny the Elder pulled the plug in his *Historia Naturalis* (AD 77): 'Observation shows that the story that the dying swan sings is false.'

But the myth lingered on. Chaucer mentions the swan 'that before his death singeth'. Shakespeare has Portia refer to 'making a swan-like end, fading in music'. Tennyson wrote a whole poem

about it. 'The Dying Swan' describes a bird whose 'warble was low, and full and clear'.

Curiously, the word 'swan' comes into English by a complex route dating back to the ancient Proto-Indo-European word *swen* — 'to sing, make sound' — which finished up being applied to a bird which doesn't.

The poet Samuel Taylor Coleridge turned the phrase on its head in the poem 'On a Volunteer Singer' (1800):

> Swans sing before they die; 'twere no bad thing
> Did certain persons die before they sing.

# Bulldog

*Bulldog is a good name for that breed, because they do look like bulls.*

Yes, they do look rather like bulls, but their name has nothing to do with their looks.

In early centuries, a favourite spectator sport was 'bull-baiting'. This 'sport' involved a bull firmly tethered, then set upon by dogs, which attacked the bull and attempted to bring it to the ground and wound its vulnerable parts, e.g. the nose. Several dogs might be involved, and an especially fierce bull could maim or kill several dogs in one 'event' by trampling, tossing or goring. Bull-baiting was very popular in Britain for several hundred years, along with bear-baiting. (In 1575 Queen Elizabeth I once watched a major bear-baiting event involving many dogs versus 13 bears.)

Samuel Pepys didn't like bull-baiting. In August 1666 he attended a bull-baiting and called it 'a very rude and nasty pleasure'.

Over the centuries it is believed that dogs were bred for bull-baiting and encouraged to have stocky bodies and solid heads and jaws which made them more successfully able to 'bait' and incite a bull to rage, whilst hopefully escaping punishment themselves. (Many didn't, and perished 'in the ring'.) Hence, the logic followed that the term 'bull dog' referred to its speciality of attacking bulls, not resembling them. The word 'bulldog' came into use in 1568 and its first known sighting in print was 1632.

Bull-baiting and bear-baiting were big business in Britain right up to the 1800s, but were banished in 1835 by the Cruelty to Animals Act.

Freed from the horrors in which they once had been forced to participate, in spite of their rather unglamorous appearance with rolling gait and glum looks, the breed known as bulldogs gradually became known as endearing pets and companions.

## Koalas

*Koalas are bears which live in trees.*

Koalas may be called 'koala bears', but they are not related to bears at all. They are marsupials, more similar in structure and habitat to opossums than to bears.

The name we use for them originated from the Australian aboriginal language of Dharuk, with a word sounding like *gula*, which was heard by English-speaking settlers as *koolah*. The first known sighting of the creatures by a European was in 1798, and by the early 1800s some settlers were referring to the tree-dwelling creatures as 'sloths' — but because of their bear-like appearance, they were also sometimes called 'monkey bear' and 'tree bear'. However, the *koolah* name prevailed, and gradually became 'koala'.

Curiously, although the koala has no relationship with bears, its scientific name refers to their resembling a bear-like animal: *Phascolarctos cinereus*. This is derived from the Greek meaning 'ash-coloured bear with a pouch'.

Because the koala appears to derive moisture from the eucalyptus leaves rather than drinking, there is a belief that the original native name means 'doesn't drink', but this is disputed by dialect authorities who explain that *gula* was simply a word applied to the animal, without any specific meaning.

# Sardines

*Sardines are little fish from Sardinia.*

'Sardines' is a very loose term. There is no specific breed of fish classified as 'sardines'. The favourites to whom the name is usually applied are pilchards when they are under 6 inches (15 centimetres) in length. But the World Health Organization's *Codex Alimentarius* of international food standards says: 'Canned sardines or sardine type products are prepared from fresh or frozen fish of:' — then come the names of 12 different species of fish, specifying that the name of the region from which the fish came must precede the word 'sardines'. They can be found in oil or no-fat-sauce sealed in tins, or can be eaten fresh, roasted, grilled or salted.

The name 'sardine' has a very imprecise pedigree. The word has been in use in English since the early fifteenth century. While it seems very likely to be somehow connected with the island of Sardinia, there are very conflicting explanations about which connection is the true one.

The name 'whitebait' is similarly unofficial. Servings of 'whitebait' in Britain, China, New Zealand, Italy, Puerto Rico and Australia may all be of differing fish species.

# Cougars

*'Cougars' are females over 35 on the hunt for connection with younger men.*

Canada is generally credited with the slang term's evolution. An internet dating site in Vancouver c.1999 was named 'Cougerdate' and reputedly encouraged opportunities for older women to meet younger men. A story circulated that the term may have been in use earlier: one of the website's founders had been told by a nephew that 'mature' women who tried to pick up fit young players from

his hockey team were known by the men as 'cougars', because the women, like the mountain lions, were in search of young defenceless animals.

By 2001, the term was in print (*Toronto Globe and Mail*, 3 March) and soon after, when Valerie Gibson's book called *Cougar: A Guide for Older Women Dating Younger Men* was published, the term took off internationally.

But since its early usage, there has been a decided shift in connotation. Initially it was something of a put-down, singling out undesirable women of 35–40-plus, who hung around bars until the end of the night, then took home whatever young drunk man was left. But over time, cougars gradually began to be perceived as purposeful and spirited women, perhaps no longer in their twenties, but attractive, possibly glamorous, and even famous.

But why cougars? Are real female cougars so liberal-minded? The Ottawa-based Canadian Geographic organisation reports that 'male cougars are polygamous ... whereas females are monogamous'.

So much for frequenting bars for multiple late-night pickups.

## Colly birds

*In the 'Twelve Days of Christmas', 'colly birds' is an old way of saying 'calling birds'.*

No, it's not. In the famous Christmas song, the fourth gift is 'colly birds'. 'Colly' is the ancient word for 'black' (still to be seen in 'colliery' and 'coal'), hence 'colly birds', which look as if they've been in a coal mine. So quite simply, they are blackbirds.

As time passed, people forgot what 'colly birds' meant, the term no longer made sense and nobody understood it. So confusion caused some people to change the word to 'calling birds' instead, though nobody understood what that meant either.

# Wolves

*Men who are playboys are called 'wolves'.*

This is rather unfair: male wolves do not 'play around'. Every wolf pack has an 'alpha male' and an 'alpha female', and they are the only two in the pack who mate and breed; and that male retains this one-female relationship for as long as his alpha-female wife is alive. It seems that male wolves are monogamous husbands: only if one of the pair dies, does the other then seek another partner.

The American National Wildlife Federation in Virginia says quite simply: 'Wolves typically mate for life.'

So — not promiscuous.

# Bears

*Bears are born formless and their mother licks the cubs into a 'bear' shape.*

This is total misinformation, born of a time when wildlife was not familiar enough to the general populace for the error to be queried. A major source of this misbelief came from the Roman author/naturalist Pliny the Elder. His *Historia Naturalis* (AD 77) states:

> Newborn cubs are a shapeless lump of white flesh, with no eyes or hair, though the claws are visible. The mother bear gradually licks her cubs into the proper shape.

The same belief remained current in Europe for at least the following 1200 years, and in 1355 is mentioned by Guillaume de Deguileville, a monk in a French abbey. His *Le Pèlerinage de l'Âme* was translated and printed in English in 1480 as *Pylgremage of the Sowle*:

Beres ben brought forthe al fowle and transformyd and after that by lyckynge of the fader and the moder they ben brought in to theyr kyndely shap.

Passing years and the eventual observations of people like Sir David Attenborough have made it clear that the belief of many centuries was in error: bear cubs are not born shapeless. When born, they look like — bear cubs!

But a hangover of the ancient belief remains in the colloquial phrase describing the organising of something not working properly into an effective condition — it has been 'licked into shape'.

## Worms

*A worm cut in half grows into two separate worms.*

It doesn't. If an ordinary garden earthworm is cut into two, you get one half of a still-alive worm and one half of a dead worm. Earthworms have a certain ability to regenerate if a cut occurs a certain distance away from the head. If so, sometimes — only sometimes — a new tail can be grown. But the cut-off tail-end of a worm has no ability to regenerate a head, and will simply die.

# under the microscope

## Heart

*The heart is on the left-hand side of the chest.*

The heart is more or less central. One ventricle can be heard more easily by listening towards the left of centre, and the aorta artery arches to the left. But a line through the middle of the body would certainly go through the middle of the heart, with only a very small portion more on the left side rather than the right.

## Fan and air temperature

*A fan in the room on a warm day makes the air more cool.*

It's an illusion. A fan doesn't actually alter the air's temperature — it just moves the existing air around and around. But the fan has doubtless been switched on because the day is warm and the room is warm. This causes some sweating, no matter how mildly, and sweat takes some of the body's heat with it. When moving air comes in contact with your skin it helps evaporate the sweat and your skin feels (temporarily) cooler. So although the fan has no major effect on the air around it, the effect of its lowering the skin's temperature can be advantageous.

If the atmosphere is particularly humid, the air already has so much moisture in it that sweat evaporates slowly, and the fan's effect on the skin is less noticeable.

An air conditioner takes heat from the air and cools it, but a fan only moves air at its existing temperature, and so can help increase the evaporation of sweat. Curiously, if the fan is electric, its motor operation may have a long-term effect of *adding* to the heat in the room.

## Lightning

*Lightning never strikes the same place twice.*

It does. NASA (National Aeronautics and Space Administration, USA) points out: 'Contrary to popular misconception, lightning often strikes the same place twice.' The same place can be struck repeatedly, especially if it's a tall, pointy, isolated object. The United States Government's National Weather Service reports that New York's Empire State Building is hit nearly 100 times a year.

## Charles Darwin

*Charles Darwin created the concept of 'survival of the fittest'.*

He didn't; he borrowed it.

Darwin's *On the Origin of Species* (1859) clarified his principles that every species develops or evolves from a previous one, by the theory of 'natural selection'. The book was studied by British philosopher Herbert Spencer, an esteemed commentator on economics, politics, philosophy, biology, sociology and psychology. He, too, was interested in evolution, and in 1864 published his *Principles of Biology*, which included his own new term 'survival of the fittest', which he compared with Darwin's term 'natural selection'. Eventually Darwin decided that Herbert Spencer's expression 'survival of the fittest' was an acceptable interpretation of his own theories, and Darwin included it in the fifth edition of his own work.

Contrary to popular belief, there was no 'the' before 'Species' in Darwin's title *On the Origin of Species*. This would have implied that he studied the evolution of just one species — human. In fact the work focused on the mechanisms of evolution, both human and non-human.

## Dark side of the moon

*Pink Floyd introduced the concept of a 'dark side of the moon'.*

Pink Floyd's famous 1973 album (estimated 50 million sold) fuelled the phrase 'dark side of the moon', although the album does contain the telling line which acknowledges that 'there is *no* dark side of the moon'. This is true: there is no dark side of the moon.

The moon revolves around the Earth and, while doing so, it is also revolving on its own axis. So one half of it appears to be dark — just as one half of the Earth is dark for approximately 12 hours out of every 24 — and the side of the moon we always see, is always the same visible side, giving the impression that the other half of the moon is always dark. A vague impression of mystery and possible danger clings to the term 'dark side of the moon'.

Forty years before Pink Floyd's offering, author Hugh Lofting had (fictionally) clarified that the moon doesn't have a dark side. Lofting's universally popular character Dr Dolittle gave us a first-hand (fictional) 'report' in the book *Dr Dolittle in the Moon* (1928), after Doolittle had climbed on the back of a giant moth on Earth, and was flown up to the moon. There he became very bouncy because of the lack of gravity, learned to talk to the insects and plants, and explored the other side of the moon:

We went onward towards the other side of the Moon — the side that earthly Man had never seen before.

And on that 'other side' Dr Dolittle discovered spring-fed pools, mysterious choir music which came from the branches of huge trees, birds taller than a man, and flowers that talked. But no darkness.

The nearest thing to night which we ever saw, was a strange kind of twilight — the slight dimming of the pale daylight which preceded a half darkness, the nearest thing to real night we ever saw on the Moon.

Thirty-one years after Dr Dolittle's moon adventure, the first satellite pictures of the moon's far side were published, and a decade later in 1968 real-life astronauts became the first men to actually see the 'far side of the moon'. And although they didn't mention musical trees or talking flowers being there, they said it certainly wasn't dark.

So ultimately the fictional Dr Dolittle, Pink Floyd and the astronauts all agree: there is no dark side of the moon.

## Aurora borealis

*Aurora borealis cannot be seen in the Southern Hemisphere.*

Aurora borealis is the name given to the light display occurring over some parts of the Northern Hemisphere in the high-altitude atmosphere. Particles originating in the magnetosphere and the 'solar wind' are directed into the atmosphere by the magnetic field of the Earth. The result is an ephemeral colourful display.

When it occurs in the Northern Hemisphere skies, it is called 'aurora borealis': 'aurora' derived from the Latin for 'sunrise', plus the Greek name for the north wind — 'boreas'.

But this colourful display is not restricted to the Northern Hemisphere. The same thing can be seen at high latitudes in southern climes: South America, Antarctica, New Zealand and Australia. Only the name is different: 'aurora australis'.

## Funny bone

*The 'funny bone' is the bone in your arm which feels 'funny' when knocked.*

It's actually not a bone, but a nerve — the ulna nerve. This nerve runs near the ulna bone and the humerus bone. It is regarded as an 'unprotected' nerve, not being buttressed by muscles or bone.

If that part of the arm is jolted, the nerve reacts with a tingling buzz sensation ... which, possibly by association with the sound of the nearby bone's name, the *humerus* bone, gave rise to the (faintly mistaken) term 'funny bone'.

## George Washington

*George Washington had false teeth made of wood.*

Researcher John Woodforde described Washington as 'suffering for most of his life from the inadequacies of eighteenth-century dental treatment' — from the age of 22 he 'lost one tooth after another'. Some of his early replacements were made from an alloy of lead, coated with wax. He lost his last natural tooth in 1796 (it is in the New York Academy of Medicine), and resorted to putting small rolls of cotton behind his lips to plump out where inadequate false teeth sat.

A surviving set of Washington's dentures is now in the National Museum of Dentistry in Baltimore, an affiliate of the Smithsonian Institution.

In 2005 NBC News announced that laser examination of the denture had been undertaken by forensic anthropologists from Pittsburgh University. This revealed that Washington's dentures included teeth of gold, ivory and lead, with implants of some human and animal teeth (horse and donkey teeth were commonly used at the time) and the base of one of Washington's dentures was hippopotamus ivory.

But there was no wood.

## Leap year

*A 'leap year' is any year divisible by four.*

Not always. Most years divisible by four are leap years — with an extra day in February.

But to keep the calendar year in line with the seasonal year, a variation occurs when a centenary year with a '00' suffix is due. A 'centenary year' may be divisible by four — but that's not enough. To be a leap year it must also be divisible by exactly 400.

For example, the years 1700, 1800 and 1900 could be divided by four — but they could not be divided by 400 — so they had no 29 February. The years 1600 and 2000 could be divided by 400, so had the extra day in February.

The next centenary year which is divisible by 400 will be 2400.

## Ground glass

*Putting ground glass in someone's food will cause them to die.*

The belief that ground glass will puncture parts of the digestive tract and cause lethal internal bleeding is unfounded.

American cardiologist and forensic scientist Douglas P. Lyle MD provides answers for medical queries and guidance for mystery murder writers. In his book *Murder and Mayhem*, Dr Lyle writes:

The glass would have to be very finely ground, or the victim would notice it as he ate. As we chew, we sense tiny pieces of gravel, sand, glass, gristle, and so forth. Salt dissolves but glass doesn't, so the food would seem gritty unless the glass had been ground into powder. But very fine glass is unlikely to cause any lethal damage to the GI tract. It would be more of a minor irritation.

Dr Lyle adds that coarser glass — broken, crushed, shards with points — *would* damage the stomach and intestines and cause internal bleeding.

But not ground glass.

## Nicotine

*Heavy smokers have nicotine stains on their fingers and teeth.*

They have stains, yes, but not of nicotine. Tobacco smoke consists of particles (which are really droplets) of different sizes, each droplet containing a mixture of organic chemicals suspended in a mixture of gases and organic vapours. Cigarettes with filters will show a colour change in the filter (from white to yellow/ochre) during the course of smoking the cigarette. This is because during the smoking process the filter is removing/trapping some of the particulate matter as the smoke passes through the filter.

Dr Steve Stotesbury, Head of Regulatory Science for Imperial Tobacco, explains that the staining of surfaces with which the smoke comes into contact, including fingers and teeth, comes from chemicals within this particulate matter. Although the particles/ droplets in cigarette smoke contain nicotine, it is incorrect to say (as many do) that it is nicotine which causes the staining. This is simply one of those myths that people are happy to accept about tobacco without giving it much thought. In fact, nicotine is colourless, and this becomes self-evident when one considers the vapour from e-cigarettes, which contains nicotine but no smoke.

# BMI

*The BMI (body mass index) shows if you are a
healthy weight.*

It might. The origin of the 'index' dates back to 1850, when its
basis was devised in Belgium by Dr Adolphe Quetelet, the director
of the Brussels Observatory. A statistician and specialist in 'social
sciences' he devised the Quetelet Index — a number describing
an individual's body mass — defined by their weight divided by
the square of their height.

The original calculation and its significance have been through
some revisions. The form currently recognised as the BMI arose
during the 1970s, in reference to the prosperity of some modern
societies being reflected in escalating weight, tending to cause
medical problems.

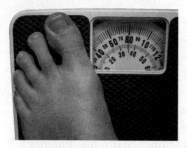

There is a consideration that
BMI was more relevant as a study
of populations, rather than for
individuals. It is recognised that
not all races in the world follow
the same BMI, and the analysis of
a BMI 'assessment' can vary from
country to country. The relevance
of the 'final figure' reached in the
equation, and where that stands in relation to a person's future
health, cannot always be the same globally. Based on studies of
health studies in various ethnicities and their genders, careful
re-calculations of the 'final figure' and its relevance have been
introduced. For example, Orientals may often be of a more slight
build than naturally sturdy Polynesians, and so the general BMI
reading would not necessarily indicate the health level of either
with accuracy.

And the weight of muscle — or the lack of it — can also provide
a factor of variation. Athletes of average height can show an
index result which is disproportionate to their actual health level.
Members of New Zealand's top rugby team, the All Blacks, can

register a BMI as high as 30, but are probably among the fittest and healthiest men in their country.

The BMI index can be a help — and possibly a guide. But it is not vouched for as an overall fail-safe decree of one's future health status. Other ways of assessing individual health in relation to body structure can include measuring the percentage of body fat present; the ratio of waist to hip; or of waist to height.

## Chicken soup

*Chicken soup can cure a cold or 'flu.*

Not quite. Medicos tend towards advising that nothing can actually cure a cold or 'flu. But in his published examination of household beliefs (*Never Shower in a Thunderstorm*), New York writer Anahad O'Connor outlines studies in 1978 by the Mount Sinai Medical Centre in Miami which showed that hot chicken soup can at least lessen some of the oppression of a heavy cold — by easing the release of mucus in the lungs, so it can be coughed up more easily. Detailed later study showed that the amino acid cysteine found in chicken protein is the solvent which aids the easier removal of mucus.

But all chicken soups are not equal. Anahad O'Connor referred to the result of studies which were published in the medical magazine *Chest*, showing that the word 'chicken' together with the word 'soup' did not automatically guarantee a lessening of bronchial discomfort. Least of all those two words in conjunction with 'noodles' and 'in-a-cup', as often seen on supermarket shelves. To be any help, it must be real chicken soup, even some of the quality canned brands.

But best of all, the invalid's soup should ideally be grandma's kind — made with a real chicken carcase and chopped onions, parsnips, carrots, turnip and celery, all simmered together for a couple of hours. Then the chicken is removed and the vegetables blended, and a dash of pepper and salt added. The outcome of that recipe gains acceptance as traditional 'Jewish penicillin' and should be welcomed by anyone suffering from a cold.

It won't cure, but will ease.

Incidentally Mr O'Connor allows that, in fact, it is wise to leave a bathtub or a shower when thunder is about, since thunder is accompanied by lightning. And lightning, while seeking a quick pathway to the ground, can travel through plumbing and water, and anyone in that water. O'Connor quotes Mr Ron Holle, a former meteorologist with the National Oceanic and Atmospheric Administration, and very experienced in tracking lightning injuries. Mr Holle reports that up to 20 people a year in the United States suffer severe shock from lightning while in the bath, or showering, or simply using a tap.

# the silver screen

## Fasten your seat belts

> *Bette Davis said 'Fasten your seat belts — it's going to be a bumpy ride.'*

She didn't. Bette Davis was playing bossy actress Margot Channing in the 1950 movie *All About Eve* and the line actually was: 'Fasten your seat belts — it's going to be a bumpy *night*.'

## 'Houston, we have a problem'

> *During the* Apollo *expedition, the remark 'Houston, we have a problem' was made.*

It's a nice neat line, but it isn't exactly what the space crew said to Houston on 14 April 1970. Their spoken report was in the past tense. John Swigeret Jnr and then James Lovell both separately said: 'Houston, we've *had* a problem here.'

Enter screenwriters Jeffrey Kluger and William Broyles Jnr, who adapted James A. Lovell's original *Apollo Expeditions to the Moon* and gave Tom Hanks the line, but changed into the present tense: 'Houston — we have a problem.'

The popularity of the movie and Hanks's authoritative delivery moved the line from its real-life beginning into this shorter and more pleasing rhythm. It is now frequently applied to any mishap which might crop up, in space or otherwise.

# Chariots of Fire

*The film title* Chariots of Fire *is a biblical quote.*

The Bible describes the departure of Elijah in a *single* chariot of fire (2 Kings 2:9) but later refers to a vision of plural fiery chariots (2 Kings 6:17).

William Blake's famous poem (1808) which became the song 'Jerusalem' retains the single chariot:

Bring me my Bow of burning gold;
Bring me my Arrows of desire:
Bring me my Spear: O clouds unfold!
Bring me my Chariot of fire!

The 1981 movie title *Chariots of Fire* invokes the plural, but when 'Jerusalem' is sung during the movie, it sticks to Blake's single chariot.

It could be called having a bet each way.

# Academy Awards

*The Academy Award 'Oscar' was named after a staff member's uncle.*

The origin of the Oscar name has been batted about for years. There have been several claimants to the name's invention, possibly spurred by the Academy's sometime denial that at the time the award was instigated there was no staff member with an uncle Oscar.

However, in 2007, British writer/researcher Philip Dodd, after travelling through the United States in his own version of Sherlock Holmes, came up with irrefutable evidence — and a real Uncle Oscar.

The original remark had come from a young librarian, Margaret Herrick, whose husband worked at the Academy. During 1931 Margaret Herrick spent time, on an informal basis, helping sort out the Academy's library. During this 'helping out' period, she saw the Academy's newish award statuette (first awarded in 1929) and made the immortal comparison with her 'Uncle Oscar'. At that time Ms Herrick was *not* a formal member of the Academy staff, hence the originally pedantic vagueness that the name was not invented by 'a staff member'. In 1936, however, Margaret Herrick did become an official staff member — and eventually rose to be the executive secretary of the entire (now powerful) organisation.

In later years, in a letter to the Merriam-Webster publishing company, she wrote that she regretted the 'thoughtless quip' because 'the Academy loses something of dignity every time the statuette is referred to as Oscar'.

Margaret Herrick died in 1946. With the help of an experienced genealogist, Philip Dodd tracked down that Margaret Herrick did have a somewhat older second cousin (referred to as 'uncle') called Oscar — her mother's aunt's son. Oscar Pierce was born in Oregon in April 1873, died in 1967. Philip Dodd spoke to his surviving niece, who described him as a kind and considerate man — of whom, alas, no photos survive.

We will never know why Margaret Herrick looked at a statuette and made a remark about it 'looking like Uncle Oscar.' But the legend that she did turns out to be true.

## The Sound of Music

*The von Trapp family escaped Austria and Nazi persecution by climbing a mountain.*

They didn't. The Baroness von Trapp's autobiography tells that they left by train in broad daylight.

# Greta Garbo

*Greta Garbo said 'I want to be alone'.*

She did — when she was playing a fictional character.

In the 1932 movie *Grand Hotel*, Garbo played the Russian ballerina Grusinskaya, who at one point said 'I want to be alone'.

Spoken in Garbo's highly individual husky voice, the line went into history — but with some confusion. An inability to recognise the difference between a character speaking lines from a script, and the real person playing the role, caused the 'want to be alone' line to be attached to Garbo herself. For the rest of her life she denied having said she 'wanted to be alone' — it was a fictional character in a film who had said it.

There is a frequently published belief that she explained the confusion by having once said that she, Garbo, wanted to be 'let' alone, but any evidence of where or when or to whom she said it is not on offer.

# Odeon

*Odeon cinemas are named after the famous Odeon in Leicester Square.*

No, the word is from the Greek: ōidē ('song') and ōideion (a building in which singing and performances took place). In other words, a Greek word for a theatre.

The word still means that in Greece. The famous Odeon of Herodes Atticus on one side of the Acropolis, built in AD 161, holds an audience of 5000 and has hosted performances by the Bolshoi Ballet, Maria Callas, Elton John, Pavarotti and Sting, as well as the Miss Universe pageant ...

The word took on new life in Britain during 1928 when entrepreneur Oscar Deutsch opened a cinema in the Midlands town of Dudley — and, using the Greek word, called it the Odeon Cinema. By 1937 Mr Deutsch had 250 cinemas called Odeons throughout Britain. They weren't named after the big one in London, because the 'flagship' Odeon Leicester Square (seating 1600) opened in 1937 — after most of the other Odeons were already up and running. But they all had a name borrowed from Greece.

## The Wizard of Oz

The Wizard of Oz *movie came 39 years after the book.*

Actually the famous 1939 movie was the third movie made from Frank Baum's book about Dorothy and the Wizard. Two years after the 1900 publication of *The Wonderful Wizard of Oz*, its story became a theatre musical, which played for six years.

The first movie of the book was in 1910, and a second movie was made in 1925 (with Oliver Hardy as one of the farmhands). Both were rather more simple than the splendid 1939 offering — which had the advantage of sound, Technicolor, and Judy Garland.

In Frank Baum's original book, Dorothy's shoes were silver, but Technicolor tempted the movie moguls to change the shoes to a brighter colour — ruby red.

# Extra-terrestrial

*Steven Spielberg invented the term 'extra-terrestrial'.*

Not at all. Mr Spielberg made a splendid 1982 movie with that name, but he didn't write it — it was written by Oscar winner Melissa Mathison. And the word she used as the title dated back over 80 years.

'Extra' = outside, 'terrestrial' = the limits of our Earth. Thus anything from beyond our normal planet. The word was first used by the famous social and science fiction writer H.G. Wells in his 1898 novel *The War of the Worlds*. The narrator of the novel tells of arriving at a pit where a mysterious cylinder has forcefully landed from above and a small crowd has gathered. The narrator is convinced that the 'Thing had come from the planet Mars' and reports:

> the yellowish-white metal that gleamed in the crack between the lid and the cylinder had an unfamiliar hue. *'Extra-terrestrial'* had no meaning for most of the onlookers. At that time it was quite clear in my own mind that the Thing had come from the planet Mars.

Robert Hendrickson's *Word and Phrase Origins* credits American author L. Sprague de Camp with the later abbreviation of 'extraterrestrial': de Camp used the abbreviation 'E.T.' in 1939, in the May issue of the magazine *Astounding Science-Fiction*.

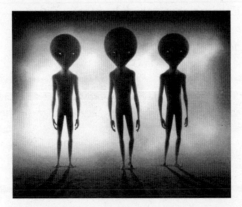

# Superman

*Superman was invented in 1933.*

The famous fictional character with super-powers was indeed first imagined by Jerry Siegel and Joe Shuster in 1933, and became a comic-strip star from 1939. But his name goes back 30 years earlier.

German philosopher Friedrich Nietzsche outlined the possibility of an Übermensch in *Also Sprach Zarathustra* in 1883. That work inspired British dramatist George Bernard Shaw, who was cautious about translating the word 'über' and settled on 'super'. Hence Shaw's play, written in 1903, was called *Man and Superman*.

Both Shaw and Nietzsche envisaged the 'super' part of their super-being to be a mental and moral strength rather than physical. Siegel and Shuster used the name borrowed from Shaw, but allied to a visual athletic image more accessible to the general public and more immediately exciting.

Their superman grew into an international icon, the central figure of countless cartoons, radio shows, films and a musical.

> The adventures of Siegel and Shuster's Superman were somewhat easier to watch than the play from which his name came ... George Bernard Shaw's *Man and Superman* lasts on stage over four hours.

# Tom and Jerry

*'Tom and Jerry' were original animated cartoon characters created by Hanna-Barbera.*

The famous cat and mouse were first seen in 1940. A year later animator John Carr came up with their names, Tom and Jerry, and a very famous duo was born.

But coupling the name Tom with Jerry wasn't new. The first known teaming of those two names was in 1821, when English sportswriter Pierce Egan published *Life in London*, the exploits of two roistering bucks named Tom and Jerry. This pair, Tom and Jerry, were constantly encountering trouble on 'rambles' and 'sprees', and the book was a great success, leading later to a stage adaptation. And to 'represent' the pair of rakes, a 'Tom and Jerry' drink was specially devised — an eggnog with both brandy and rum. The 'Tom and Jerry' drink survived well into the following century, and is a prominent part of Damon Runyon's 1932 story 'Dancing Dan's Christmas'.

There is supposition, but no real evidence, that the 'Tom and Jerry' drink was still well enough known nine years after Damon Runyan's story that it occurred to animator John Carr as catchy names for two rascals ... names which had been in circulation for over a hundred years.

There would seem to be little connection between Egan's London dandies and Simon and Garfunkel — but that duo's original name in 1957 was Tom and Jerry.

# persons of influence

## Helen of Troy

*Helen of Troy was the most beautiful woman in the world.*

She might have been, bearing in mind the limited view in ancient times of what constituted 'the world' — and if Helen ever existed at all.

The first writing about her which we know of is in Homer's *Iliad* c.800 BC. But Homer's awareness of Helen came from hearing much older tales about her, dating from the Helladic period, at least 300 years prior — which is when she is believed to have existed. So 'awareness' of her beauty and her perceived connection with the Trojan wars has only filtered to us through several millennia.

There has long been close and serious study concerning the location of Troy. By the time of Ovid's poem 'The Heroines' (c.30 BC) its supremacy had long faded: 'Now there are fields of corn where Troy once was.'

Further certainty about its place and time varies — the UNESCO World Heritage Committee places it in the Turkish province of Çanakkale.

In the long-standing belief about Helen of Troy's beauty and the impressive duration of military mayhem which her beauty caused, one detail about Helen only very rarely arises — the circumstances of her birth. The legend about that brings an unwelcome doubt to modern minds that Helen may be a figure of mythology and did not actually exist at all. Greek legend places her in an exalted line of aristocracy — as a daughter of Zeus the chief god — from whom there was no higher level of descent. But wait: the legend continues that in order to seduce Helen's mother, Leda, Zeus had assumed the form of a magnificent macho swan. His seduction was successful — there was connection, conception, and there was issue. Leda produced swan eggs, *from one of which Helen emerged!*

It's somehow difficult to come to terms with the concept that a baby who was half-bird, and born out of a swan's egg could be anything but seriously disabled, let alone stunningly beautiful. But there is comfort in the awareness that legend is more easily believed than fact — and is often preferred.

## Sir Edmund Hillary

*Sir Edmund Hillary said he climbed Everest 'because it was there'.*

He did say that. But he didn't originate the line.

He was quoting eminent mountaineer Sir George Mallory, who had said it in 1924, after attempting to reach the peak

but not making it. Sir Edmund had no intention of pretending he had invented the laconic remark. A mountaineer himself, he was surrounded by other mountaineers, all of whom knew the Mallory line and recognised it as a quote. But the reporter who publicised Sir Edmund's reply (in 1953) did not realise that Hillary was quoting a respected predecessor, and mistakenly attributed the line to Hillary himself.

## George Washington

*George Washington said 'I cannot tell a lie'.*

There is no evidence that the 'chopping of the cherry tree' and its aftermath ever happened.

In 1800, after Washington had died, Mason Weems, the author of a George Washington biography, put out the story that six-year-old George had hacked into a cherry tree in the garden (not actually chopped it down), and when the following day his father demanded to know who had done this damage, the child immediately owned up — and earned the father's praise for his honesty.

According to Weems's version, the incident happened over 60 years before (if it happened at all), and supposedly was told to him by the only witness — an (unnamed) old lady who claimed to have been present at the chopping, the discovery, the questioning, and the answer.

The story is regarded as apocryphal, an invented myth, bolstered somewhat by Weems's reputation for his forthright imagination. (For example, his self-penned biographic credentials included having been 'former rector of Mt. Vernon Parish', but that parish never existed.)

## Winston Churchill

*Winston Churchill was bottom of his class at school.*

When he was seven years old, at his first school, Churchill was indeed bottom of the class.

Churchill went to three schools, then military college. At seven years old he was sent to a boarding establishment run by a sadistic headmaster, who at the slightest perceived 'offence' gave the boys savage canings on their bottoms, until blood (or more embarrassing eruptions) occurred. Winston was punished frequently. Dispirited with beatings, and worried about pleasing his father, he became over-anxious and nervous before exams, and failed miserably. All letters home were vetted, so he was unable to tell his parents what was happening.

When his parents did find out about the regime of constant beating, he was immediately withdrawn and sent to a happier institution. About which he later wrote: 'There was an element of kindness and sympathy which I found conspicuously lacking in my first experiences.'

His school work began to improve. Biographer Mary S. Lovell points out that when he was 14 and moved to Harrow School, 'his reports were above average'. At 18, Churchill entered the Royal Military College, Sandhurst, and quickly gained even better reports. He graduated from Sandhurst in the top 20 (from a class of 130), and received his commission from Queen Victoria as a second lieutenant when he was 20 years old.

So yes, he had been bottom of a class briefly and was being caned until he bled. But history shows that after that he wasn't held back for very long.

## Florence Nightingale

*Florence Nightingale had great influence in the cause of professional nursing and the respect due to it.*

True. But she had a strange attitude to her own health. After returning to London in 1856 from her pioneer war work in Turkey, Miss Nightingale was received by Queen Victoria and Prince Albert. Then she went to her bedroom — and stayed there.

It is not, and never has been, clear whether Miss Nightingale had developed a genuine medical condition or had a neurotic estimation of her own state of health. From 1857 onwards she remained either in her bed or on her bedroom couch. Important people came to call, she wrote a book, and maintained constant and voluminous correspondence — but it all happened in the bedroom.

She contributed reports to the Royal Commission on the Health of the Army; raised funds for the Royal Buckinghamshire Hospital in Aylesbury; wrote the book *Notes on Nursing*; advised the American government on organising field medicine and inspired the volunteer body of the United States Sanitary Commission; encouraged a commission of enquiry into conditions in the British Army in India; and was closely involved in establishing a School for Nurses at St Thomas's Hospital. She inaugurated training for midwives and reforms in the workhouses of the poor in England and Ireland, and was consulted to give advice on matters of well-being to appointed viceroys heading to foreign parts. *Encyclopedia Britannica* reports that: 'All these works were accomplished by a woman generally supposed to have died.'

She didn't die until 1910 — just over 50 years since she took to her bed and couch, and never left them. Having five servants in the house had been a help.

# Napoleon

*Napoleon was ambitious, powerful — and very short.*

There is disagreement about this. During the 1800s the British 'inch' (2.54 centimetres) differed from the French *pouce* (2.71 centimetres), so references to the height of Napoleon in French terminology (5 *pieds* 2 *pouces*) were mistakenly seen in British context as 5 feet 2 inches, whereas, taking the difference in measure systems, it was actually 5 feet 7 inches (1.70 metres). British historian Robert Wilde points out this was 'no shorter than the average Frenchman'.

Wilde also points to the autopsy of Napoleon by a French doctor Francesco Antommarchi, who entered the height on his report — but the autopsy was signed off by British doctors, who may have misinterpreted the '2 *pouces*' as the equivalent of 2 British inches, which it wasn't.

And also the Emperor's nickname, '*Le Petit Caporal*', could be understood literally as 'small', but *petit* can also be used as a term of affectionate regard (in the same way as *mon vieux* can mean 'my good friend', not just 'my old person').

So the least that can be said is that Bonaparte might have been shorter that our twenty-first century image of an idealised powerful military man — but by how much is far from clear.

The statue of Napoleon in the Duke of Wellington's London house is 6 feet 3 inches (190 centimetres) tall, and built rather like an entrant in Mr Universe — which one judges as rather fanciful. But it seems likely that in real life Napoleon was exactly the same height as Tom Cruise, so it can't be said that 1 metre 70 centimetres is any barrier to success.

# it's in the book

## The Mad Hatter

*The Mad Hatter is a character in* Alice in Wonderland.

There certainly is a hatter in *Alice in Wonderland* and in *Through the Looking Glass,* and the dormouse does whisper to Alice just once that the hatter is 'mad'. But at no time is the character ever called The Mad Hatter.

## Frankenstein

*Frankenstein was a man-made monster.*

No, he wasn't. Victor Frankenstein was a (fictional) Swiss chemistry student in the novel *Frankenstein; or The Modern Prometheus* by Mary Shelley.

The story tells that for two years Victor Frankenstein experimented with ways of creating artificial life out of inanimate matter — and succeeded in creating a man-like 'humanoid'. The humanoid had no name, but is referred to as 'fiend' or 'daemon'. When Victor Frankenstein loses control of the humanoid, the consequences are disastrous.

The Frankenstein story was rejected by two publishing companies but accepted by a third; after being published in 1818, it has become one of the most famous fantasy-fictions in the world.

## William Shakespeare

*Shakespeare is a great English playwright.*

Indeed, yes. But it's not quite clear that we're spelling his name correctly. There are only six known signatures written by Shakespeare himself, and each one is spelt differently:

Willm Shaksp
William Shakespe
Wm Shakspe
William Shakspere
Willm Shakspere
William Shakspeare.

Not one of these matches up with 'Shakespeare', the spelling universally used in referring to him.

## 'Elementary, my dear Watson'

*Sherlock Holmes said 'Elementary, my dear Watson'.*

Sherlock Holmes never said it. The line does not appear in any of the 60 Holmes stories written by Sir Arthur Conan Doyle. Holmes certainly said 'elementary' and often spoke to 'Watson' — but he never put them together into 'Elementary, my dear Watson.' Curiously, it was P.G. Wodehouse who did.

In a 1909 Wodehouse novel called *Psmith, Journalist*, Psmith mentions 'a necessity to unlimber his Sherlock Holmes system' and murmurs 'Elementary, my dear Watson'. Conan Doyle still had 19 more years of genuine Sherlock stories to come, but he is not known to have commented on Wodehouse's neat contraction and never used it himself. Twenty years after Wodehouse, the line appeared in the 1929 movie *The Return of Sherlock Holmes* — and has been in common use ever since.

Agatha Christie offered a jokey version in 1937, when Hercule Poirot says: 'How do you say ... "obvious my dear Watson?" ' (*Murder in the Mews*).

Many people believe it to be a quote from Sir Arthur Conan Doyle, but not so!

## 'Pride and prejudice'

*Jane Austen created one of the most memorable phrases in English.*

She certainly made it famous, but Jane Austen didn't originate the neatly contrasting phrase 'pride and prejudice'.

She was going to call her book 'First Impressions', but biographer Paula Byrne reports that Jane admired Fanny Burney's much earlier novel *Cecilia* (1782) in which the character of Dr Lyster announces firmly several times that the other characters' miseries have been caused by 'pride and prejudice'. Jane Austen's eye was caught by the phrase, so she renamed her book *Pride and Prejudice* (1813). Both the book and the phrase have remained famous for 200 years.

## Desiderata

*'Desiderata' is an inspiring reflection dating from 1642.*

It was believed to have been 'dated back to 1642 and found in a Baltimore church'. But no, its opening words — 'Go placidly amid the noise and haste ...' — and all its other words were written by an American lawyer and poet called Max Ehrmann, who copyrighted it in 1927. Apparently Mr Ehrmann used his prose poem 'Desiderata' on his annual Christmas cards, but did not add the copyright symbol there.

People liked the poem, passed it around, one thing led to another, and in 1959 the poem crossed the path of the Reverend

Frederick Kates, rector of Old St Paul's Church, Baltimore. He found the piece inspirational, and decided to circulate it among his congregation. It was printed out on church paper with the heading 'Old St Paul's Baltimore AD 1692'. The date 1692 was a standard part of the church's address, that being the year it was founded, but casual readers interpreted that as the year of origin of the poem.

So 'Desiderata' and the legend of its seventeenth-century origin grew. And grew even more when prominent American politician Adlai Stevens died in 1965 and 'Desiderata' was found by his bedside. The poem went international.

The copyright on 'Desiderata' was renewed by Ehrmann's widow, and inherited on her death by a nephew, who onsold it to a publishing company.

In 2010, a bronze statue of Ehrmann was unveiled in Terre Haute, Indiana, his hometown.

'Desiderata' is Latin for 'things that are yearned for and desired', and the prose poem still retains its gentle impact. Several celebrity recordings and an enormous number of posters and wall hangings keep its message alive.

Some 'take-off' comedy versions have arisen — not the least, a vernacular offering from Australian icon Dame Edna Everage. Her version was of course named 'Desednarata': 'Go placidly, possums, into the rat race ...'

# Ruth

*Ruth stood among the alien corn and wept.*

This image comes from 'Ode to a Nightingale' by Keats. Without Keats actually saying so, there has long been an impression that Ruth and the alien corn are a reference from the Bible. Keats wrote:

> Perhaps the self-same song that found a path
> Through the sad heart of Ruth, when, sick for home,
> She stood in tears amid the alien corn ...

The lines are beautiful, and famous, but Bible scholars fail to see how Keats could condense the biblical book of Ruth into such brief imaginings. There is no biblical evidence of Ruth being doleful, the term 'alien corn' is never mentioned in connection with her, nor the sound of a nightingale.

Professor Viswanatham, a specialist in comparative poetics at Andhra University, India, comments:

> These lines from the *Ode to a Nightingale* are said to refer to the Bible story by all annotators and critics. But a doubt arises if Keats's Ruth is the same as the Bible Ruth. Keats's Ruth is sad, sick for home, in tears, amid the alien corn. The Bible Ruth is neither sad nor sick for home nor in tears. As far as the Bible story goes, even 'alien corn' is inapplicable.

# Romeo and Juliet

*'Wherefore art thou Romeo?' Juliet wants to know where he is.*

Juliet is alone (on her balcony) when she says this, so it could seem logical that she might wonder about Romeo's whereabouts. But that isn't the meaning of 'wherefore' at the time the play was written (c.1594).

The 'wherefore' here means 'why' rather than 'where'. Juliet is concerned — quite rightly — about the feud between her Capulet family and Romeo's Montague clan. She is asking, 'Romeo, why are you a Montague?' Their love is impossible because of their family names, and she asks him to change his allegiance, or else she will change hers.

> O Romeo, Romeo! wherefore art thou Romeo?
> Deny thy father and refuse thy name;
>  Or, if thou wilt not, be but sworn my love,
> And I'll no longer be a Capulet.

## 'It was a dark and stormy night'

*'It was a dark and stormy night' is a comic line invented by Snoopy the dog in Peanuts cartoons.*

Snoopy certainly gave the line considerable exposure, always using it as the opening line when writing one of his novels — but not getting much further.

Snoopy's creator, cartoonist Charles Schultz borrowed the line from the novel *Paul Clifford* by acclaimed nineteenth-century MP and prolific writer Lord Edward Bulwer-Lytton (left). Less acclaimed in following centuries, Lord Bulwer-Lytton's writing may have faded to obscurity but for Schultz's whim. Starting in 1965, Schultz's character of the engaging dog Snoopy frequently sat on the roof of his kennel hammering out yet another novel on his toy typewriter, always beginning with 'It was a dark and stormy night ...'.

Somehow those seven words epitomised the formality and ponderous pace which characterised Bulwer-Lytton's writing.

This is the original line:

It was a dark and stormy night; the rain fell in torrents — except at occasional intervals, when it was checked by a violent gust of wind which swept up the streets (for it is in London that our scene lies), rattling along the housetops, and fiercely agitating the scanty flame of the lamps that struggled against the darkness.

# Miss Havisham

*Miss Havisham was an ancient crone.*

Miss Havisham's actual age is never mentioned in *Great Expectations*, but there is a good clue given when young Pip is sent to her to 'play' and entertain her. Pip's age isn't given either, but he is consistently referred to as 'boy', and he tells us that at this time he was too young to be formally 'apprenticed' to Joe the blacksmith. So when he met Miss Havisham he would be somewhere under 14. Miss Havisham became a total recluse on the day of being jilted while dressing for her wedding. She tells Pip she has 'never seen the sun since you were born' — thus setting her wedding 14 years earlier at the most. It would be normal for a Victorian maiden (especially a rich one) to marry in her early or mid-twenties, so when she met Pip she could have been between 35 and 40 *at the most,* and when he grew to be 21 she would have been no more than 47.

The concept of Miss Havisham being truly ancient is reinforced by the crumbling surrounds in which she lives — and even more by the magnetic performance of actress Martita Hunt in the famous 1946 movie. Her moth-eaten context and eccentric characterisation brought Dickens's original description to life with such impact that she set the benchmark for most people's image of Miss Havisham for many years after. But Martita Hunt was in fact just 47 when she played Miss Havisham — Dickens would have approved.

# Diamonds are forever

Diamonds are Forever *is a James Bond book title written by Ian Fleming.*

It certainly is, and was published in 1956. But the title isn't exactly original. It's a tweaking of a line originally written in 1947 by New York advertising woman Frances Gerety on behalf of De Beers

Consolidated Mines. It became a key element in the advertising of their diamonds, and in 1999 won an award as 'advertising slogan of the century'.

Ms Gerety's line actually read 'A diamond is forever', a not-so-subtle implication that diamonds don't deteriorate, which increased their suitability for engagement rings or wedding presents.

Ian Fleming moved the slogan into international James Bond territory with a subtle alteration of 'a diamond' into the plural.

Nor did Ian Fleming coin the phrase 'Never Say Never'. American songwriter Harry MacGregor Woods was ahead of James Bond in 1935, with his song 'I'll Never Say "Never Again" Again' recorded by the Boswell Sisters and by Ozzie Nelson.

## Gone with the Wind

Gone with the Wind, *one of the most famous book titles in the world, was dreamed up by Margaret Mitchell.*

Except that she didn't write the title.

The Pulitzer prize-winning novel (1936) sold 30 million copies, and the subsequent blockbuster movie (1939) is still regarded as one of the classics of all time. It was this that moved the expression 'gone with the wind' into front-line attention. Author Margaret Mitchell had plucked one line from a poem which had been published 40 years before, and she made that line world-famous. The poem (1896) by British poet Ernest Dowson has the forbidding title '*Non Sum Qualis Eram Bonae Sub Regno Cynarae*' but contains the more accessible line: 'I have forgot much, Cynara! gone with the wind' ...

Besides being Mitchell's title, the line occurs in the novel when Scarlett O'Hara is wondering if her home Tara is still standing.

Ms Mitchell had reputedly considered several other titles: 'Bugles Sang True'; 'Not in Our Stars'; and 'Tote the Weary Load'. In hindsight it's easy to agree that *Gone with the Wind* was a better choice.

Cole Porter was also apparently a fan of the same Dowson poem. In Porter's show *Kiss Me Kate*, the characters of Bill and Lois sing 'Always true to you, darling, in my fashion', echoing a sentiment from *'Non Sum Qualis'* in which Cynara is told repeatedly: 'I have been faithful to thee, Cynara! in my fashion.'

> Incidentally, MGM's highly publicised search to find a screen Scarlett O'Hara culminated in choosing Vivien Leigh, one of the great beauties of the time. This decision was at quixotic variance with writer Margaret Mitchell's opening line: 'Scarlett O'Hara was not beautiful ...'.

## James Bond

*'James Bond has turned 50!'*

Headlines in 2012 proclaiming this 'fact' appeared to be calculated only in reference to Bond on-screen. But the Bond character had appeared in Fleming's books since 1953 and on TV screens in 1954 (in *Casino Royale*). Clearly the '50' applied not to the date of Fleming's original creation of the character, but to his first appearance on the *movie* screen – which was 1962. Examination of Bond's bio in Fleming's books reveals that James Bond's 'actual' birth seems to have been in 1924, but there could be some understandable resistance to headlines proclaiming 'James Bond has turned 90!'

Estimating the age of fictional characters is fraught with potential disillusion if one takes fictional characters seriously. Most of them were presented as fully grown when they first appeared in literature, so it would be a reasonable assumption that their birth was at least 20 years earlier. By that reckoning, Sherlock Holmes was born in 1867, Tarzan was born in 1892, both the Lone Ranger and Superman in 1913 and Batman in 1919.

Imagination and movie commercialism promote their image as being eternally young and vigorous.

The born-20-years-before-publication system falls apart with Dr Who (first seen in 1963 but supposedly born several hundred years earlier) and Mickey Mouse — first seen in 1928, but certainly not 20 years old at the time.

It's probably best just to accept fictional characters at the age they appear to be now.

## Not a penny more, not a penny less

*'Not a penny more, not a penny less' was Jeffrey Archer's description of financial see-saws.*

The catchy title of Lord Archer's novel (first published in the United States in 1975) was in fact borrowed from George Bernard Shaw's play *Pygmalion*. Eliza Doolittle's dustman father, Alfred, discovers that his daughter Eliza is now staying in Henry Higgins's house — the plan being that there she will learn better English. Alfred misinterprets and mistrusts this relationship and insists that her presence in the house must be paid for — to him. Doolittle tells Higgins: 'You give me what I ask you, Governor: not a penny more, and not a penny less.'

## Sherlock Holmes

*Sherlock Holmes wore a deerstalker hat and smoked a curved meerschaum pipe.*

Arthur Conan Doyle never said so — nor are they mentioned in the Holmes stories. According to Holmes's creator, he smoked an 'old oily clay pipe' (in 'The Red-Headed League') and occasionally one made of briar. And Dr Watson mentions him wearing an 'ear-flapped travelling cap' ('The Adventure of Silver Blaze') but not necessarily a 'deerstalker'.

Sidney Paget was the artist commissioned by *Strand* magazine to illustrate the early Holmes stories (from 1891), and it was he who imagined Holmes in a deerstalker hat and drew him accordingly.

In 1899 actor William Gillette appeared in the first play centred on the Holmes character, and besides consistently wearing the deerstalker hat which the artist Paget had invented, also introduced a curved meerschaum 'calabash' pipe to the character (possibly because its curved shape made it easier to speak lines clearly while the pipe was in his mouth). Gillette played the Holmes role 1300 times on stage, and then in an early Sherlock Holmes movie (1916).

The hat-and-pipe image has remained in over 200 movies since, featuring 75 different actors playing Holmes.

So in spite of its not being part of Conan Doyle's concept, the dual image of deerstalker hat and curved pipe has become part of the collective consciousness. It is even on the wall tiles which announce the London Underground station at Baker Street, where Holmes (fictionally) lived.

# on the map

## Hawaii

*Hawaii is in the South Pacific.*

Perhaps capitalising on the new-found glamour in the title of the Broadway show and hugely successful movie, during the 1960s a spate of advertising invited tourists to sun-filled attractive beaches and gently waving palms, where they could: 'Holiday in the South Pacific Paradise of Hawaii.'

Hawaii truly is a genuinely attractive destination — except for one little glitch ... Hawaii isn't in the South Pacific. It's in the North Pacific (which somehow doesn't sound as good).

## Christopher Columbus

*In 1492 Christopher Columbus discovered America.*

To be exact, there is doubt about how this should be worded.

Scandinavian legend has it that the discovery of America was some time in AD 1001 by Leif Eriksson, who, according to *Encyclopedia Britannica*, was 'certainly a member of an early Norse Viking voyage to America' (meaning the 'North American continent', since his landfall and visit are believed to be in what we now call Canada). And strictly speaking Columbus didn't reach what we know as America at all. He arrived and set foot on what we now call the Bahamas, and was unaware of the large mainland.

Speaking even more strictly, Columbus cannot be credited with 'discovering' even the Bahamas: the people native to that area (and America) had been living there long before Columbus arrived.

## The Antipodes

*Australia and New Zealand are the Antipodes.*

Care is need with the word 'antipodes'. Its actual meaning (from Greek) is 'opposite the feet', thus from one's footprint straight down through the centre of the Earth and out the other side — but at what place?

Britain frequently refers to Australia and New Zealand as its 'Antipodes' — blissfully overlooking the fact that Britain's 'opposite feet' are actually standing in water — the Pacific Ocean. Australia's 'opposite feet' are also in an ocean — the North Atlantic — and New Zealand's 'opposite feet' are in Spain, Portugal and Morocco.

Britain and Australia are not the only nations with antipodean oceans: the opposite feet of mainland United States are in the Indian Ocean; and Japan's feet are in the South Atlantic.

## Kilt

*The kilt is a garment originated by the Scots.*

The Scottish kilt is recognised worldwide as a distinctive garment style. But if the kilt is defined as 'a knee-length type of male skirt', then that isn't a Scottish invention. Males wearing skirts have cropped up in the history of many parts of the world through centuries past, before trousers became a norm. Spain, Iraq, Ireland, Egypt, France, Greece, Rome, Bulgaria, Albania — and others —

all have a 'male skirt' somewhere in their history. The passage from any of these into historic Scotland is open to wide dispute.

But to whatever part of international history it is distantly related, Scotland's pleated tartan kilt has certainly outclassed all the others in universal perception.

## 'MADE IN USA'

*Goods labelled 'MADE IN USA' must come from America.*

There is a Japanese town called Usa, hundreds of years old, in the Prefecture of Oita. The town is home of the Usa Shrine, built in the eighth century — and it has never pretended to be in America. International practice requires that imported manufactured goods identify the *country* of their origin, not just a town. Customs officials would have been unlikely to miss noticing that goods labelled 'MADE IN USA' were actually being imported from Japan.

## Aboriginals

*Aboriginals are natives of Australia.*

Yes — and everywhere else.

The Latin *ab+ origin* means 'original inhabitants of *any* land', so people native to any area are aboriginals. In Australia, custom and usage have modified the term into 'Aborigine', but without changing the basic meaning.

# Middle Earth

*J.R.R. Tolkien invented the term 'Middle Earth'.*

He didn't. The phrase 'middle earth' is a very old expression, dating back to ancient Scandinavian mythology and drifting into Anglo-Saxon English originally as *middangeard*. It is mentioned in one of the oldest pieces of English writing, *Beowulf*, possibly dating from the eighth century. Tolkien was a professor of Anglo-Saxon studies, so was familiar with *Beowulf*, in which *middangeard* was perceived as a mystic place, somewhere between Heaven and Hell.

Shakespeare refers to it in *The Merry Wives of Windsor*, when someone speaking about Falstaff says 'I smell a man of middle-earth', indicating that it is not a very desirable place. This shows only that the name of the place was a known factor before *The Lord of the Rings* was first published in 1954. But Tolkien only took the name. He certainly invented the language, the settings, the characters and the stories.

# Siamese twins

*Twins joined together at birth are known as 'Siamese twins'.*

This is a geographical misnomer, since the 'original' — or rather the first famous — set of joined twins were actually Chinese-Malaysian. They were born in 1811 to a fisherman and his wife in Thailand, and were known there as 'Chinese twins'. Taken to America and exhibited as curiosities, their description subtly changed to 'Siamese twins' — possibly because they were actually born in Siam (Thailand), but also perhaps because 'Siamese' sounded more intriguing than 'Chinese'. The twins married sisters and had 21 children between them. They died within an hour of each other. In contemporary times, the description 'Siamese' is rarely heard, the accepted description now being 'conjoined twins'.

# Tulips

*Tulips come from Holland.*

They certainly are found in Holland, in their thousands. But tulips are not native to the Netherlands; they were taken there from Turkey and central Asia, where they are native, and there are other members of the tulip family indigenous to Africa. The bulbs started drifting from Turkey across Europe in the mid-sixteenth century, and some may have arrived in the Netherlands into private gardens. But in 1593 the Netherlands University of Leiden had tulips planted in the university's botanical centre; consequently, 1594 is regarded as the 'official' date of first flowering of this attractive bloom in that country. Further cultivation led to a frenzy of popularity known as 'tulip mania', and the eventual establishing in the Netherlands of tulip-growing as a major industry. But there's no escaping that the flower is actually of Turkish origin: the name 'tulip' is an anglicised version of its name in Turkish — *tülbend*, meaning 'turban', since the bloom has a resemblance to a Turkish turban.

# Ferdinand Magellan

*Ferdinand Magellan was the first person to sail right around the globe.*

It seems nit-picking to say he wasn't, but the truth is that Magellan never got right around the globe. Through no fault of his own, he missed the last 16 months of the full global journey.

In 1519 on behalf of the King of Spain, Ferdinand Magellan as captain, leading five ships, set out from Seville to find a sea route 'to the west' and to spice trading. The travelling was fraught with difficulties and deaths — storms, mutiny, desertion and wreckage. But after eight months' arduous sailing and with two ships already lost, Magellan and the three remaining ships reached what we now call the Philippines. There, trouble arose. Rajah Humabon, a local aristocrat with whom Magellan established friendly terms, persuaded Magellan to attack a rival noble, Lapu Lapu, on another island. In the resulting battle, Magellan was killed by the natives' very effective bamboo spears.

The three surviving ships set off to continue their voyage. One ship burned and another leaked so badly that she could not continue. After two leaders replacing Magellan had died, the command was taken over by Juan Sebastián Elcano.

This remaining ship, with Elcano in command, sailed for another 16 months and arrived in Spain in September 1522 ... three years after its departure.

The King of Spain ordered a coat of arms to be designed, containing a representation of the globe and a motto which read *Primus circumdedisti me* ('You went around me first'). It was presented to Juan Sebastián Elcano — the first man to have led a ship around the globe.

## Desert

*A desert is an area of the Earth's surface where it is too hot for normal living.*

On the contrary: the Arctic, the Antarctic and parts of the Himalayas are classified as deserts, and are anything but hot! The important factor is rain — or rather the lack of it. The formal definition of a desert is: 'A region that is devoid or almost devoid of vegetation because of low rainfall — insufficient to support human habitation.'

## Sarah Palin

*Sarah Palin said 'I can see Russia from my house!'*

Sarah Palin, when Governor of Alaska, once described Alaska as a neighbour of Russia, and said 'You can actually see Russia from land here in Alaska.' Which is perfectly true — the Alaskan island of Little Diomede is only a few kilometres from the Russian island of Big Diomede, behind which the coast of mainland Russia can clearly be seen.

But during the 2008 American presidential campaign, comedy actress Tina Fey, dressed up to look very like Sarah Palin, in a scripted satirical fake TV interview changed the words to: 'I can see Russia from my house.' Ms Fey was so convincing that many people believed they'd heard Sarah Palin say it — which she hadn't.

## The Great White Fleet

*The visits of the Great White Fleet were a display of American goodwill.*

Everyone thought that, but 93 years later the Australian Government revealed doubts.

The Great White Fleet was an impressive American convoy of 16 battleships plus escorts, staffed by 14,000 sailors, sent by President Theodore Roosevelt on a peaceful circumnavigation of the world in 1908–9. They visited 20 ports in six continents with a disarming display of goodwill combined with a very public demonstration of America's growing military strength.

In 2001, the government of Australia's Foreign Affairs, Defence and Trade Group revealed that in the context of international politics in 1908, 'goodwill' wasn't the only purpose of the Fleet:

In the event of a crisis between the US and Japan, Britain's ally, Australia and New Zealand, as loyal dominions of the British Empire would be potential enemies of the United States.

Roosevelt felt it necessary to ascertain the sentiments of Australia and New Zealand.

On a more practical level, Rear Admiral Sperry, the commander-in-chief of the fleet ordered that during the fleet's visits intelligence be gathered to compile war plans for the capture of New Zealand and Australian ports.

And:

Thus, when the fleet arrived in each Australian port to a tumultuous welcome, its intelligence team went to work compiling detailed reports on the defences and infrastructure of each city as part of invasion plans. The hospitality of the local population undoubtedly made it easier for the fleet's officers to gain insight into Australia's strengths and weaknesses, and probably direct access to the information necessary to prepare plans to capture the new nation's major cities.

The resulting reports, having been lodged with the American Department of the Navy, then went into storage. While it is clear that the extremely hospitable reception the Fleet received in the Pacific was a clear demonstration of the friendliness of people in this area towards America, the report concludes:

However, the mere compilation of the plans was an acknowledgment of what US national interest might dictate could happen to Australia in the event of hostilities between the US and Japan.

Parliament of Australia, *Foreign Affairs, Defence and Trade.*
*Report on ANZUS after 50 years* (28 August 2001)

An international tour of goodwill? Maybe ...

# Bali Ha'i

*Bali Ha'i can be found in Tahiti.*

Since the book, the musical and then the movie *South Pacific*, many places have claimed to be Bali Ha'i. Twenty-three years after James Michener published *Tales of the South Pacific*, he set the record straight about where this magic place actually was: first by writing in the *Philadelphia Sunday Bulletin* (1970, kept in the James A. Michener Library at the University of Northern Colorado), and later in his own memoir *The World is My Home* (1992). Michener made it clear that Bali Ha'i doesn't actually exist.

In the Second World War, while serving in the Solomon Islands, Micronesia, Michener arrived in a small native settlement on the island of Mono, 640 kilometres north of Guadalcanal. There he saw a cardboard sign tacked to a tree giving its name: Bali Ha'i. Intrigued by the name, Michener 'borrowed a pencil and in a soggy notebook jotted the name against the day when I might want to use it for some purpose'. Later, when stationed on Espiritu Santo island in Vanuatu, he could look out to a distant island which appeared across the sea to be smooth-looking, hazy and peaceful. That island was Ambae — and its peaceful look was somewhat illusory, since Michener later wrote that it was 'steaming and savage' and that 'no sane person would willingly visit'. (Ambae is dominated by an impressive volcanic cone, still categorised as active. It last erupted in 2005, and is believed to be among the world's most dangerous volcanoes.) However, as a writer he combined the visual effect of the distant, shapely island with a name from 1000 kilometres away, and created from them a peaceful image of loveliness and imagination.

But his 'creation' was never an actual place. The name from a distant settlement in the Solomons which Michener thought he 'might want to use ... for some purpose' had a use found for it — merged with the distant vision of Ambae in Vanuatu.

So in the scenes supposedly showing Bali Ha'i in the 1958 movie — what place *were* we seeing? We were watching a total composite: footage of the island of Tioman in Malaysia, plus Kaua'i and Mount Makana (Hawaii), possibly a few seconds of Tahiti (this has been disputed), and indoor studios in Santa Monica Boulevard, Los Angeles (for the boar's tooth dance ceremony).

As a real place, Bali Ha'i doesn't exist. But Michener's fanciful image became the new 'Shangri La' ... and one of the music world's most familiar and haunting songs.

## Flushing the toilet

*Toilet flushing goes in a different direction depending on the hemisphere.*

The clockwise or anti-clockwise movement of natural phenomena is described as the 'Coriolis effect'. This applies to very large areas of water and air, but does not impose 'directional flow' on very small amounts — such as when the plug is pulled in a kitchen sink containing water or when a toilet is flushed. In such cases there are two governing factors: the shape of the receptacle holding the water, and the way the water is released into it. These form the direction the water takes when it flows out, wherever you are.

The rumour that some companies in the Southern Hemisphere, in order to placate homesick immigrants, have designed special toilet pans which flush the same way as toilet pans in the Northern Hemisphere is indeed just a rumour — and a myth. It was begun by a highly amusing episode of the TV series *The Simpsons*, where the family travelled from the United States to Australia — to confirm whether toilets flushed in a different direction from those in their hometown of Springfield.

## Pacific Ocean

*Magellan named the Pacific Ocean.*

He did, but inspired by an early optimism rather than a fuller acquaintance.

Magellan came around the southern tip of South America in November 1520, and entered the waters to the west of Tierra del Fuego on what must have been a good day, as he referred to the area as '*Mar Pacifico*' — the 'Calm Sea'. Things didn't go well for Magellan after that, but the name stuck — not entirely appropriately. While the Pacific Ocean can often be as calm as when Magellan first saw it, rough waters are not uncommon and its vast area is capable of tempestuous outbursts. Severe turbulence, cyclones (aka hurricanes and typhoons), tsunami, gales and depression storms can cause havoc and make the ocean anything but *Pacifico*.

Magellan didn't get it quite right.

## Country names

*Nations are never named after a real person.*

AMERIGO VESPUCCI

Some nations take their name from a legendary figure (perhaps mythical) or a long-ago saint, but several nations are named after a single real person.

For instance, America is named after Amerigo Vespucci, whose first name appeared on a map showing known areas of that country in 1507, and has remained there ever since. Columbia is named after Christopher Columbus, and Mauritius after Prince Maurice of Nassau.

Bolivia is named after Simón Bolivar, who led the country away from Spain into independent nationhood. Bermuda is named after Juan de Bermúdez who 'discovered' the islands in the 1500s. The Philippines' name is a commemoration of King Philip II of Spain. The Seychelles were named to honour French politician Jean de Seychelles.

Kiribati is the local version of 'Gilbert', as in Captain Thomas Gilbert, and the Marshall Islands are named after Captain John Marshall.

Saudi Arabia takes its name from King Ibn-Saud, and Liechtenstein from its royals, the Princes von und zu Liechtenstein.

The Solomon Islands are named after a biblical character depicted there and in the Koran as real: King Solomon, to whom gold was brought (1 Kings 9:28).

# festivals and saints' days

## St George

*St George, the patron saint of England, was English.*

Fanciful supposition that St George might have been born in England is counterbalanced by rather less fanciful supposition that he wasn't.

Very little, almost nothing, is known for sure about St George. The first known historical reference to him was 200 years after he'd died. This refers to his dying in Turkey in AD 303 when he was about 30 years old, in an era and a country where communication and literacy were nowhere nearly as well developed as in later centuries — so stories which spread about him became more and more enhanced.

His birth is widely disputed. Some accounts have him born in Turkey, but there is also a belief that he was born c.AD 275 in Israel, 15 kilometres south of Tel Aviv, to Greek parents. As a young man he became Christian. After travelling to Turkey, he joined the Turkish branch of the Roman army there, and rose to being a respected officer. But the Roman Emperor Diocletian announced that Christianity was not acceptable among his troops. George, a devout Christian, refused to renounce, so was tortured and lacerated with swords, but still he refused and was executed in Izmit in Turkey in the year 303 on the day we now call 23 April.

Christianity was then still in its very early stage of development, but stories of George's martyrdom spread rapidly, far and wide, and were immeasurably embroidered as they grew. One of the most famous stories describes his encounter with a dragon. This story has so many versions and embellishments that it is impossible to sort out a coherent narrative.

The most popular version tells that when George was in Africa — and history is silent about what he was doing in Africa — he came to a town where a dragon had taken up residence in the local spring. The locals couldn't get water, and the dragon refused to eat offerings such as a sheep, and would eat only human flesh, so a person had to die each time the locals needed fresh water.

George came travelling by and saw a young woman tied to a rock with her long girdle, awaiting the dragon to come and eat her. George chivalrously rescued her, fought the dragon and vanquished it, then tied the woman's girdle around the dragon's neck and led it into the city, along with the young still-alive woman. As a result, 15,000 people from Libya were so impressed with George that they became Christians overnight.

Other enhancements avow that the young woman was a princess and that George actually killed the dragon.

Did it happen? Nobody knows, but it seems unlikely since dragons don't actually exist — though to be fair, one version of the story says it was a crocodile. In following centuries, many fanciful poems and paintings and statues have depicted versions of this story — and it is mainly from those that we get our impressions of George, not from historical facts.

George's exploits and his nobility of martyrdom, enhanced or not, became extremely popular talking points throughout Europe and further afield. In the year 494 he was made a Catholic saint, and interest in him and stories about him and people seeing visions of him continued to grow.

English soldiers rampaging through Europe on Crusades reputedly heard tales of him, and spread the word around their homeland about this legendary brave martyr. Some early desperate attempts were made to claim him as an Englishman — as the son of Lord Albert of Coventry — and to assert that the famous dragon was slain at Dragon's Hill in Oxfordshire, which is all quite odd since he was apparently born where Israel's main international airport now stands, and there is no evidence that he ever went to England.

Nevertheless, in 1344 King Edward III of England made St George the patron saint of England and patron of the English Order of the Garter. Shakespeare mentions him in *Henry V* (1599) in the famous 'Once more unto the breach, dear friends', which finishes with the cry 'upon this charge / Cry "God for Harry, England, and Saint George!" '

His Catholic sainthood was later diminished, but he is still often referred to as 'St' George.

He is patron saint of England, Portugal and Malta (among many other places); of soldiers, archers, Boy Scouts, sheep, butchers and agricultural workers; and for protection against leprosy ... and syphilis.

St George's 'military insignia' — a red cross on a white background — became part of every British soldier and sailor's uniform, and is part of the red-white-and-blue cross design on the British flag.

# Easter

*Jesus died on Good Friday.*

Who knows? There is no certainty about when Jesus was born. But his death is described as being related to the festival of Passover, which is still celebrated by Jewish people all around the world on its actual date. So the calendar day of Jesus' death could easily be worked out each year, in line with the dates of Passover, when he is reported to have died.

But in the year AD 325 a committee meeting was held in Turkey in the town of Iznik (formerly called Nicea), and a system was worked out whereby the death of Jesus could be commemorated — not on the actual anniversary of his death, but always on a weekend.

The committee's decree: 'Easter Sunday is the first Sunday after the first full moon after the [Northern Hemisphere] equinox.'

So the date of Easter can vary by almost six weeks. The earliest date Easter can occur is 22 March and the last date is 25 April.

## St Valentine

*St Valentine is identified with romantic love.*

Nobody knows why! There seem to have been two men called Valentine canonised; both commemorated on 14 February. But any reliable evidence about their lives and actions connecting them with romance is thin to the point of invisibility. One thing known about them with any certainty is that both were Roman Catholic priests — thus having no experience whatever with romantic love, engagements or being married.

As usual when no reliable evidence exists, fantasy stories abound. Ancient Rome had the 'Lupercalia' and 'Februa' festivals of purity, health and fertility during the month we now know as February. One 'story' had the youths and maidens of Rome during this festive period drawing at random a name from slips placed in the opposite gender's jar, thus these slips were said to be the forerunner of 'Valentine cards'. Alas, no link has ever been established between the February festivals and the 'Feast of St Valentine' — and the random names-from-jars gimmick didn't begin until several hundred years after 'Lupercalia'.

The first known link between the Valentine gentlemen and any form of romance comes from Chaucer in 1382. But the romance is (literally) for the birds! Chaucer's *Parlement of Foules* tells us:

> For this was on Saint Valentine's Day,
> When every bird cometh there to choose his mate.

Over the following 200 years, St Valentine gets scant mention — George Gascoigne in 1577 refers to 'saint Valentines day' simply as part of the calendar. But by 1593 Thomas Nashe was making a closer association between the saint and young lovers:

> It was the merie moneth of Februarie
> When yong-men in their iollie roguerie
> Rose earelie in the morne fore breake of daie
> To seeke them valentines so trimme and gaie.
> With whom they maie consorte in summer sheene ...

Shakespeare chose a midstream position. In *A Midsummer Night's Dream* he adheres to the aerial association:

> 'Good morrow, friends. Saint Valentine is past:
> Begin these wood-birds but to couple now?'

But eight years later, in 1603, he changes tack when Ophelia — and not a bird — has a romantic thought:

> Tomorrow is Saint Valentine's day,
> All in the morning betime,
> And I a maid at your window,
> To be your Valentine.

None of the above writers' references dwell on, or even mention, boxes of chocolates and expensive roses.

But sometime after 1603 the fragile fantasy became fuelled through the rise of mass media and was re-shaped by rampant commercialism. The ancient, unknown (and totally bachelor) saints Valentine became the focus of a huge commercial sell-out – aggressively encouraging people to spend, spend, spend ...

# Halloween pumpkins

*Carved pumpkins with a light inside are a traditional part of Halloween.*

They have become so, but the actual genuine tradition was rather less colourful.

Many of the rituals associated with Halloween ('All Hallows Eve') have their origins in Ireland and Scotland, and an ancient holy-day called Samhain. It was believed that a gate to the 'Other world' opened just for that night (31 October – 1 November), allowing fairies and spirits to roam freely. York University historian Nicholas Rogers, in *From Pagan Ritual to Party Night*, describes the period as one of 'supernatural intensity, when the forces of darkness and decay were said to be abroad'.

When Christianity became influential, the Samhain observance gradually morphed into 'All Hallows Eve', the night before All Hallows Day — the day of honouring all saints, known and unknown.

Among the various customs attached to early Samhain (and which passed over to Christian All Hallows) was the making of 'jack-o-lanterns', inspired by the slightly weird flicker of light which sometimes occurred over peat bogs. The lanterns were traditionally made from a swede or mangelwurzel, hollowed and carved into a stark face, and candlelit from within.

Irish emigrants who travelled to a new life in America during the 1800s naturally wanted to continue their old customs. The problem with Halloween jack-o-lanterns was that traditional turnips and mangelwurzels — freely available in Ireland and Scotland — at that time could not easily be found in America. Hence the change to the more commonly available pumpkins,

which were already a colourful feature of American 'harvest festivals' and were large and easy to carve.

By the mid-1800s, the American pumpkins had moved into commonly being featured as Halloween jack-o-lanterns. From then on, immense commercialisation of the pumpkins-as-Halloween-symbol spread their imagery onto every conceivable product (even 'Halloween chocolates' with pumpkin-flavoured centres!). The more humble turnip, basis of the genuine traditional lantern, was eased into distant memory.

## Santa Claus

*Santa Claus comes from the North Pole.*

No, he comes from Turkey. The mythical figure of Santa is built on the image and reputation of Nicholas, a revered Turkish bishop. Nicholas was born during the fourth century in Patara on the Gulf of Makri in Turkey, and lived his whole life in that country. A Christian, he worked according to the principals of Jesus, and rose in the ranks to become Bishop of Myra (now called Demre). A statue stands there to commemorate his memory, and relics believed to be of Nicholas are preserved in the Antalya museum, in Anatolya, Turkey.

In later centuries, legends about his kindness to children, and the help and comfort he showed towards poor families, led to his being revered across Europe. He became known to the people as 'Saint' Nicholas, although he was never actually canonised. His 'sainthood' was extended to being 'patron saint of children and sailors'.

Dutch people in particular honour him, and hold a St Nicholas parade each year. When many people emigrated from the Netherlands to America, they presented their annual St Nicholas parade just as they had done at home. American author Washington Irving's *History of New York* (published in 1809 and 1821) refers to the image of St Nicholas in fanciful tone, and makes inventive mention of his 'riding over the tops of the trees, in that self-same wagon wherein he brings his yearly presents to children'.

In the transition from stately St Nicholas to jolly Santa Claus, the decisive factor came in 1823. On 23 December 1823, *The Troy Sentinel*, a small New York newspaper, published an anonymously submitted poem — 'A Visit From Saint Nicholas' — with the opening line: ' 'Twas the night before Christmas, when all through the house ...'. Later revealed as being written by Clement Moore, the poem established images which Moore simply invented — the chubby figure, the fur-trimmed jacket, beard, sleigh, chimney visit — and rather importantly, eight reindeer.

During the annual St Nicholas parade in New York, a reporter asked who the stately figure in bishop's robes represented and was answered by a Dutchman giving the Dutch version of the bishop's name — *Sinterklaas* — which the American journalist mistakenly wrote down as 'Santa Claus'. The legends about Nicholas and his generosity began to be attached to this new name — Santa Claus.

In 1863 the image of the benevolent old man and his sleigh which Clement Moore had created, appeared in a black-and-white drawing, with him working on toys to give away as gifts. From then on the totally re-adjusted version of St Nicholas as Santa Claus became a major international industry.

But he had never heard of the North Pole ... or Coca-Cola.

# music and song

## 'Lord of the Dance'

*'Lord of the Dance' is an Irish song.*

Afraid not — the tune was composed in 1848 by a Shaker elder in America, Joseph Brackett.

It was heard mainly only in America until 1963 when English poet Sydney Carter set words to it. He was inspired by his private view of Jesus 'as the incarnation of the piper who is calling us', and he gave this newly worded incarnation of the old tune a new name: 'Lord of the Dance'. Curiously, although created by an American and an Englishman, it has a distinctly Irish sound, and is now more widely associated with Ireland than with anywhere else.

## Bloody Mary

*'Bloody Mary is the girl I love.'*

Bloody Mary was a real-life person, known to James Michener when he was a Lieutenant Commander in the US Navy.

Michener's book *Tales of the South Pacific* told of his days in the US military in the Second World War's Pacific area, and the people around him at the time. When serving in Vanuatu he met a local character whom he later immortalised as 'Bloody Mary'.

The reading public learned of her in 1947 when Michener's book was published.

Bloody Mary became known to a much wider audience in 1949 when the musical of Michener's tales was transformed into a Broadway show *South Pacific*, and then became a worldwide hit. The 1958 movie of the musical brought an even greater audience.

The character of Bloody Mary was originally played in New York and also in the movie by Juanita Hall, and in London by Muriel Smith. Both ladies were African-American, and other productions worldwide tended to cast a buxom African-American or a rounded and lively Polynesian as an insouciant and outspoken Bloody Mary.

But wait a minute — was the real Bloody Mary a war-time version of Aunt Jemima?

Not at all. In Michener's words, far from being a black-and-buxom life of the party, Bloody Mary was repulsive and repugnant; her few teeth were jagged and black, tinged with yellow; she dressed sloppily; her face was lined with betel-stained grooves; and she was notably foul-mouthed.

Nor was she black or Polynesian. Bloody Mary came from a village outside Hanoi towards the Chinese border, so she was Vietnamese.

The line in the script saying so was discreetly dropped from many productions during the 1960s and 1970s.

Now ain't that too damn bad!

## 'Here Comes the Bride'

*The bride came down the aisle to Wagner's 'Here Comes the Bride'.*

It's probably Wagner's best-known melody worldwide, but the original doesn't have anything to do with a bride *approaching* her prospective husband waiting for her and the ceremony.

In the opera *Lohengrin* from which the music comes, the famous chorus occurs *after* the wedding ceremony — as the lady attendants escort the newly married Elsa to the wedding chamber, advising her of the earthly joys which await when she joins her new husband there.

And in strict Christian terminology, the bride doesn't come down or up the aisle — that central part in a church is properly called the nave.

## Bluebirds and Dover

*'There'll be bluebirds over,
the white cliffs of Dover ...'*

No there won't be, and never have been.

In 1941 American song-writers Walter Kent and Nat Burton had never been to Britain, but they composed a song sincerely intended as a morale-booster for British people during the grim days of the Second World War. And with that endearing quality which Americans have, they assumed everything outside America was — or at least should be — the same as it is back home.

But the bluebird is native to America, and has never been seen at Dover, or anywhere else in Britain. Nevertheless, when conveyed by the magic voice of Vera Lynn, the song became one of the most enduring icons of the war years. Taken literally, the song could unfortunately be seen to mean that the war would never end, since bluebirds have not yet flown over Dover. But the British completely disregarded that and took the song to their hearts in exactly the spirit it had been intended — a graceful paean of hope.

Birds which are a beautiful blue do exist ... but there is an element of rarity about them. In 1908, Maurice Maeterlinck wrote a story about a boy and a girl who were seeking a visionary blue bird, which to the children represented happiness. Twenty-six years later, in 1934, Sandor Harmati, Edward Heyman and Harry Parr-Davies composed the song 'Bluebird of Happiness', recorded by the famous tenor Jan Peerce. By 1939 the bluebird image was further established by those 'happy little blue birds' which flew over Judy Garland's rainbow.

Maeterlinck's story was filmed a number of times — the most prominent being the 1940 version starring Shirley Temple, and the 1976 version starring Elizabeth Taylor, Jane Fonda, Ava Gardner and Robert Morley. But the enormous success of Jan Peerce's recording did more to consolidate Maeterlinck's image of the bluebird representing happiness than either of the movies. The bluebird continues to be an acknowledged symbol of happiness — even if they never fly over Dover.

## 'Auld Lang Syne'

*'Auld Lang Syne' was written by Robbie Burns.*

He didn't write it — either words or melody.

Burns was an expert on the old folk poetry of his beloved Scotland, and he also had a fine ear for music. One day during a country walk, Burns heard a very old man sing a quavering version of an ancient Scottish dialect term — *auld lang syne* — which had been known in Scotland for over a hundred years. But Burns realised that the old man's song had never been 'taken down', so he set to work to expand the phrase into five verses based around the old saying 'auld lang syne' (which has a meaning roughly equating to 'the good old days').

Burns's expanded version of the brief piece he heard the old man singing fitted rhythmically into one of the many ancient 'folk tunes' which abounded in countryside and village, and were even occasionally 'borrowed' for use in formal opera and concert instrumentals. His adaptation of an enlarged ancient verse allied with a pleasantly 'accessible' folk tune was an example of his genius in respecting the moods of ancient Scottish folklore, and making them available to a wider public. 'Auld Lang Syne' was not published until after Burns died, but its 'wider public' then rapidly became very wide indeed.

The song has been recorded over a thousand times and is sung by literally millions of people on New Year's Eve.

## The 'Marines' Hymn'

*The 'Marines' Hymn' is an American song.*

Not entirely. The tune was plagiarised from the famous French composer Jacques Offenbach's opera *Geneviève de Brabant* (1867).To this tune, American words were added from the book *Rhymes of the Rookies — Sunny Side of Soldier Service* by W.E. Christian (1917).

'Hail Hail the Gang's All Here' is a similar hybrid: the tune is stolen from Gilbert and Sullivan's *Pirates of Penzance* (1879), onto which the 'gang' words were added by American 'tinpan alley' lyricist Theodora Morse in 1917.

## 'Jingle Bells'

*'Jingle Bells' is a favourite Christmas song.*

Strange — because it never mentions Christmas or anything to do with Christmas. The song has no connection with December, having been composed in 1857 for the American festival of Thanksgiving in November.

Nobody knows why the song gradually moved towards December popularity, and is now widely sung around the world by many people who have never seen a one-horse sleigh (or snow).

## 'I'll Take You Home Again, Kathleen'

*'I'll Take You Home Again, Kathleen' is a lovely Irish song.*

It's a lovely American song and has no connection at all with Ireland.

Thomas Westendorf was a teacher at an organisation for juvenile offenders in Hendricks County, Indiana. He was an accomplished violinist, singer and part-time composer. A great many of his songs were published in the late 1800s, but only one of them became known all around the world.

It happened because two songwriters he knew — Arthur French and George Persley (real name George Brown) — together composed the song 'Barney, Take Me Home Again' in 1875, and they dedicated the song to their friend Thomas Westendorf . He was intrigued with the song's story: a wife (not named) asking her husband Barney to take her back home to the place she'd come from (not named).

Oh Barney dear, I'd give the world
   To see my home across the sea,
   Where all the days were joy imparted
   Before I went to roam with thee.

So Westendorf set out to write a companion version — a husband promising his wife that he *would* take her home. He chose the name Kathleen for the pining wife and placed her somewhere (not named) far from the place she came from (also not named). The result in 1876 was 'I'll Take You Home Again, Kathleen'.

The effect the song had was phenomenal. Westendorf's song became — and still is — an international favourite.

Henry Ford asked for an autographed copy; Thomas Edison loved it and wrote to Westendorf to tell him so. Over the decades, many top-line performances have been recorded: by Bing Crosby, Joseph Locke, Mitch Miller, Johnny Cash, Slim Whitman, Elvis

Presley — and it even made it onto *Star Trek,* sung by Lt Col. Kevin Riley (Bruce Hart).

The curious thing is that, although the song was written in America and makes no mention of Ireland, an illusion grew, and kept on growing, that Kathleen's 'home' was Ireland! This has become so firm in folklore that Irish performers sing it convincingly as being part of their heritage, and published collections of 'Irish music' often include 'I'll Take You Home Again, Kathleen' — an all-American song.

> The Monte Carlo Philharmonic Orchestra and vocalist Robert White recorded *The Favourite Irish Songs of Princess Grace of Monaco,* and along with 'Mother Machree' and 'Galway Bay' is — 'I'll Take you Home Again, Kathleen' ...

## The stately homes of England

*'The stately homes of England' was a term of Noël Coward's.*

Not originally. Sir Noël borrowed the line from a poem written by Felicia Hemans in 1827:

> The stately Homes of England
> How beautiful they stand,
> Amidst their tall ancestral trees
> O'er all the pleasant land.

One hundred years later, Coward used Ms Heman's line to start his satirical version of her poem:

> The stately homes of England
> How beautiful they stand,
> To prove the upper classes
> Have still the upper hand.

## Tiger by the tail

*The song 'Hold That Tiger' is about 'holding a tiger by the tail'.*

'Tiger Rag' is a famous instrumental jazz standard, first recorded in 1917, with no vocals. Fourteen years later Harry DeCosta added the 'Hold That Tiger' lyrics, which became a huge hit for the Mills Brothers in 1931.

But the song isn't about a real tiger. Alan Lomax, biographer of Jelly Roll Morton, tells how it's about playing poker:

> in barrelhouse lingo, 'tiger' meant the lowest hand a man could draw in a poker game — seven high, deuce low, and without a pair, straights or flush. It takes nerve to hold onto a tiger and bluff it to win.

'Bucking the tiger' and 'twisting the tiger's tail' both also occur in card-playing slang.

Metaphors referring to a tiger can be traced to 1829 — 'To get hold of a tiger by the tail' — and a Chinese version from 1875: 'He who rides a tiger is afraid to dismount.' Both indicate being in a situation which is difficult to get out of: whatever you do will be disadvantageous.

But no real tigers were involved in the making of the song 'Hold That Tiger'.

## The 'Hallelujah' chorus

*People stand for the 'Hallelujah' chorus because at the London premiere the King stood up when he heard it, thinking it was the national anthem.*

It's a nice story, but has two major flaws. In 1743 there was no such thing as a British national anthem. 'God Save the King' didn't become respected as a national anthem until about 1825.

Nor is there any evidence that King George II attended the 1743 London premiere of *The Messiah* by Handel (right). A doubtful letter written 37 years later claims the King was there, but if so nobody else seemed to notice, and it is not recorded in the court circular.

There is information from 1750 that 'some' people were standing for the 'Hallelujah' chorus, and more information from 1756 that the 'crowd' was standing *for the big choruses* — plural.

But the reason for standing in the 'Hallelujah' chorus is completely unknown, although the impulse firmly remains.

# Bagpipes

*Bagpipes are uniquely Scottish.*

They are certainly an eminent factor in Scottish tradition, lifestyle and international image — but unique to that country? No.

For many centuries goatskins fitted with dried river reeds or hollowed-out animal bones drilled with holes have been part of village music for herdsmen, shepherds, festivals and social rituals in so many parts of the world that it is impossible to say exactly where the evolution of bagpipes actually began.

Embryonic versions were widespread. Musicians in ancient Egypt played their *zumarah*, other bagpipe ancestors and later relatives were known in the Arabian Peninsula, the Aegean, Caucasus, Bulgaria, Poland and Russia. France had its *cornemuse* and 'bellows-blown *musette*', Breton featured the *biniou*, Germany and Scandinavia had the 'union pipe', and Ireland its *Uilleann* pipes, Spain its *gaita gallega* and Italy the *zampogna*.

There are references to bagpipe-type instruments in ancient Greek and Latin. Roman armies marched to war inspired by bagpipe music. In rural Italy an ingenious version of the ancient instrument can still be seen

— powered by blowing into a car tyre's inner tube adapted for musical use. Some translations of the Bible use the word 'bagpipe' to describe its ancient ancestor, when people are called to a golden statue set up near Babylon (Iraq):

> at the moment you hear the sound of the horn, flute, lyre, trigon, psaltery, bagpipe, and all kinds of music, you are to fall down and worship the golden image that Nebuchadnezzar the king has set up. (Daniel 3:5)

It was a long and convoluted world tour, but the bagpipe reached the zenith of its evolution and dignity after arriving in Scotland.

## 'The Star Spangled Banner'

*Puccini used the American national anthem in* Madama Butterfly *to signify that Butterfly's lover was an American.*

He couldn't have, because when *Madama Butterfly* was composed in 1904 America didn't have a national anthem at all.

'The Star Spangled Banner' was first heard in the early 1800s and gradually became popular in some contexts. Sporting events played it for patriotic-type openings, and in 1889 the American Navy played it when flag-raising, but the song had no official status in the nation.

Nobody really knows why Puccini chose those few dramatic bars of a completely unofficial song to indicate the nation of America, but it was a fortunate choice. The song did become America's national anthem in 1931, 27 years after *Madama Butterfly* premiered.

Ever since, audiences and critics have referred to the opera's music including some stirring bars of 'the American national anthem' when in fact the song had no Congressional standing in Puccini's time. 'Hail Columbia' and 'My Country 'Tis of Thee' were its competitors for 'national anthem' status.

And ... whisper it: the 'Star Spangled Banner' tune, which Puccini grafted into *Butterfly*, is not even American. It's a British tune composed by John Stafford Smith, former organist in the Chapel Royal in London.

## Tipperary

*'It's a Long Way to Tipperary' is a famous Irish song.*

Actually no, it was composed by English music-hall singer Jack Judge, who had never been to Ireland.

Jack Judge overheard a man saying to a companion 'It's a long way to ...', and, although he didn't properly hear the destination, out of the blue and for no known reason Jack's mind filled in the word 'Tipperary' — a place he'd never seen, but the name seemed to fit the rhythm forming in his mind. So he composed a song about what a long way it was to get there, and sang it onstage the next night in the Stalybridge music hall. This was in January 1912.

Within two years, the song had grown into a minor hit — but greater fame was on the way. Within the British Army there was one battalion whose members were mostly from Ireland: the 7th Battalion, Connaught Rangers Regiment. Many of them had been stationed in Tipperary and knew that town well; some had sweethearts there. The entire battalion took up singing 'It's a Long Way to Tipperary' in the barracks, and taught it to all newcomers.

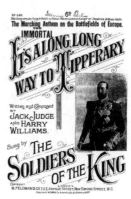

In 1914 after the declaration of what became The Great War, the Connaught Rangers were among the many British troops who went to battle. Each of the regiments as they marched sang its favourite song, such as 'Soldiers of the Queen Are We' or 'Goodbye Dolly, I Must Leave You'. The Connaught Rangers sang 'It's a Long Way to Tipperary'.

A London journalist standing in a street in France had never heard 'Tipperary' before — but the words 'It's a long way to go' seemed to sum up the image of young men marching in foreign fields to a war they didn't really want to be in. His despatch to London mentioned only one song: 'Tipperary'.

From then, the song's fame grew. 'Tipperary' overcame all barriers, and was sung and enjoyed by military and civilians alike throughout the war. Many had their spirits lifted by the cheerful optimism of the Irish-sounding song.

Chinese war workers in France sang it, eventually Germans sang it, too. When peace arrived, the song went home with troops from Canada, Australia, India and New Zealand.

In Ireland, the town of Tipperary welcomed the attention and pragmatically accepted that its name had been made world-famous — by a man who'd never been there.

## 'How Great Thou Art'

*'How Great Thou Art' is a well-known British hymn.*

It's totally Swedish. Known in Sweden as '*O Store Gud*', the tune is an old folk melody and the words were penned by Swedish preacher Carl Boberg in 1885.

In 1925, a version of the hymn in English was translated by Professor E. Gustav Johnson in America as 'O Mighty God', but did not make the impact of a later translation by English missionary Stuart Hine. He heard the Swedish song being sung in Russian when he was travelling in Poland, and he, too, made a new English translation with the title 'How Great Thou Art'. In 1949, with some adaptations to words and tune, Hine's version of the song was published in a gospel magazine which was sent to 15 countries.

It became the most popular hymn in the BBC's 50-year season of *Songs of Praise*. In America the hymn featured prominently in Billy Graham crusades, and Elvis Presley won two Grammys with his two recorded versions (1967 and 1974).

# Edelweiss

*'Edelweiss' is a genuine Austrian folk song.*

It isn't. 'Edelweiss' was composed in 1959 by Richard Rodgers, to words by Oscar Hammerstein, and sung by Theodore Bikel in the musical *The Sound of Music*, starring Mary Martin. Its popularity was immediate and far-reaching, enhanced even further by the later movie, when it was sung by baritone Bill Lee (dubbing for Christopher Plummer) and Julie Andrews.

So convincingly did the song evoke exactly the image it was seeking — identity with the Austrian countryside — that a vague assumption grew that it was genuinely a song from Austria. Under that illusion, the United Methodist Women's Conference of America issued a set of words for a Christian benediction, to be sung to the tune of 'Edelweiss'. The result was so appealing that other denominations took up the idea, and the new benediction sprouted across America as freely as edelweiss on a mountain-side. Lawyers for the estates of Rodgers and Hammerstein were obliged to remind the churches that the use of copyright material could result in legal action.

American writer Mark Steyn, reviewing the book *Enchanted Evenings* in 1997, explained that:

> 'Edelweiss' from *The Sound of Music*, is invariably assumed to be a real Austrian folk song, indeed, a few years back, the White House went further, playing it at a state banquet for the Austrian president, under the impression that it was the country's national anthem.

Mr Steyn may have been correct in his observation that many people thought 'Edelweiss' was the real Austrian thing. But he must have misheard the 'national anthem' rumour, which appeared to have surfaced in 1984, when President Kirchschläger of Austria visited the White House, and the real Baroness von Trapp was among the guests. The Reagan Presidential Library shows that, when speaking of America's relationship with Austria, President Reagan said:

> At one point in *The Sound of Music*, the character who plays Baron von Trapp sings a song about the edelweiss, an Austrian flower. And before the song ends, the lyrics become a prayer for Austria itself. It is a prayer Americans join in — and bless your homeland forever.

So a presidential seal of approval — but not a national anthem.

## Snake-charmer's music

*A snake-charmer's flute music fascinates the
snake and lulls it into a 'swaying dance'.*

Snakes have no ears — they can't hear the flute. There is a 'sensory perception' built into their system, mainly through the bones, which conveys a recognition of some vibrations which could be classified as 'sound' — but not the complexity of music.

It's believed that the swaying of the charmer's flute is the more influential factor in the snake's behaviour. Far from being fascinated, the snake perceives the swaying flute as a possible enemy and moves in a watchful ready-to-attack manner. But it's a safe snake ... most 'charmer snakes' have had their venom glands removed, or their teeth. In some cases the snake's mouth has been stitched so that only the tongue can dart in and out.

# Happy Birthday

*'Happy Birthday' is an old folk song for children.*

It's not a 'folk song'. Folk songs generally aren't under copyright, but 'Happy Birthday' is.

In 1893 there were three Hill sisters in Louisville, Kentucky. Two of them taught at the local kindergarten, and Mildred Hill put together a simple little tune, to which sister Patty added eight simple words for lyrics. It was intended, and used, as a welcoming song to be sung by the teacher each morning:

Good morning to you, good morning to you,
Good morning, dear children — good morning to all.

Later in 1893, their song was copyrighted and published in a book of songs for kindergartens. The song was popular and gradually spread further than Kentucky — sometimes substituting the words 'Happy Birthday' instead of 'Good Morning'.

Without the sisters' permission, the original tune was then re-published with new 'Happy Birthday' words. By 1924, radio was gaining attention and movies were beginning to take hold. In 1931 'Happy Birthday' appeared in the Broadway show *Band Wagon*, then became a 'singing telegram' for Western Union in 1933, and surfaced again in Irving Berlin's show *As Thousands Cheer* in 1934.

Noticing all this, Jessica, the third Miss Hill, believed that since her sisters owned the tune, they should have the credit — and some profit. Jessica Hill went to battle.

In 1934 Jessica was able to establish legal copyright to her sisters for their melody. Singing telegrams immediately stopped offering it, and a theatre play used a character speaking the words (which aren't copyright) to avoid using the tune (which is).

The present-day royalties are administered by rigidly observant copyright owners — and must be paid if the song is ever part of a profit-making enterprise. To use the song in a movie or television show can cost $25,000, and charges apply for its being heard in a stage performance (payment required for *each performance*), and when the tune is incorporated into toys, music boxes, watches, advertising, mobile phones, birthday cards which 'sing', and even 'musical underwear'.

Composer Leonard Bernstein's show *On the Town* and the Boston Symphony were both hit with copyright warnings and had to withdraw using the 'Happy Birthday' tune in a 'commercial context'. As did Igor Stravinsky.

'Happy Birthday' has been named in the *Guinness Book of Records* as one of the three most-sung songs in the English language, along with 'For He's a Jolly Good Fellow' and 'Auld Lang Syne', neither of which is in copyright and can be sung anywhere, anytime, without charge.

But legal changes in the American copyright system make the 'Happy Birthday' tune still under copyright in any commercial context until 2030.

Its royalties bring in a large income every year, and a BBC documentary during 2012 on *The Ten Richest Songs in the World* unhesitatingly put 'Happy Birthday' at No. 1, having made 'significantly more money in its time than any other song' ... a total of more than £30 million (over US$48 million).

This does not rule out its being sung privately, as it is at thousands of children's parties. When your daughter turns five or grandma turns 80, singing 'Happy Birthday' at a party in your house is fine. But if you plan to sing it anywhere which is being broadcast on radio or television, or has a ticket price at the door, then it might be as well to ensure your bank account is in good enough shape to pay the 'copyright bill' which will arrive.

# myths and legends

## William Tell

*William Tell shot an apple off his own son's head.*

There is no evidence that William Tell ever existed.

The date usually given for his marksmanship and his later joining the rebellion against Austrian suppression is 1307–8. But no mention of him can be found until over 150 years later in *White Book of Sarnen* by Schreiber (1475), and in a song which reached print in 1501.

The major focus of the Tell legend (or myth) was *Chronicon Helveticum* by Tschudi, published in 1734. This version of the story became an accepted source for the *History of the Swiss Federation* in 1780, and also caught the attention of Friedrich Schiller, whose play *William Tell* (1804) became the basis of the Rossini opera (1829).

So the ball was truly rolling, aided by the opening music from Rossini's opera becoming the best-known overture in the world – launching, since 1933, every episode of *The Lone Ranger* (2900 radio episodes, 220 TV episodes and six movies).

But alas, legend and folk songs and *The Lone Ranger* aside, the fact remains that historians can find no actual evidence that William Tell or Governor Gessler ever existed, and legends about acute marksmanship with crossbows crop up in several other places.

England's folklore tells of William of Cloudeslee, whose arrow could split an apple from his son's head 400 yards away. Denmark had the archer Palnatoke, forced by King Harald to shoot an apple from his son's head — while the boy was running. And in Scotland a legend tells of a marksman called Black Patrick shooting an egg off his son's head.

Whether William Tell actually could shoot an apple from a boy's head, and even whether he was a real person, is still disputed — and unproven.

## Finger in the dyke

*A Dutch boy saved Holland by plugging*
*a leaking sea-wall with his finger.*

The story has no basis in fact, but was a popularly published might-have-been by various authors in Britain and America. Eleven different versions existed before 1865, when American writer Mary Mapes Dodge's novel *Hans Brinker, or The Silver Skates* was published. Within her book, there is a separate story called 'The Hero of Haarlem' — about a boy who finds a dyke-wall leaking, and stays all night with his hand plugging the leak, until adults find him in the morning, and rush to do repairs. Outstripping the previous 11 versions of that (fictional) story, Mary Mapes Dodge's novel made 'the boy and the dyke' universally famous — even though the story wasn't true, and the boy was often confused with her book's main character Hans Brinker (who was not the boy at the dyke).

After *Hans Brinker*, several other full-length books emerged

"Do you still believe only you can save the Lowlands?"

telling amplified stories about the brave boy who 'saved Haarlem' (or sometimes the whole of Holland!).

Mary Mapes Dodge had never been to the Netherlands, but visited there some time after her book became so successful (eventually there were five different movie adaptations). She discovered that people in the Netherlands had taken with stoic calm the fanciful publicity about something which had never happened. Indeed, very sensibly, the Netherlanders erected statues of the fictional dyke-plugging boy in three different places where the fictional dyke-damming hadn't occurred. The tourists love them.

## Pink and blue

*Traditionally, pink is for girl babies, blue for boys.*

Pink for girls and blue for boys is comparatively recent ... traditionally, it was the other way around.

Until well into the twentieth century, many cultures — including British and American — followed a 'tradition' that boy babies wore pink and girls wore blue. (France didn't — their girls wore pink — which outside France was regarded slightly quizzically as 'a French fashion'.) Pink for boys and blue for girls somehow developed as accepted parenthood practice. The June 1918 issue of the *Ladies Home Journal* explained that:

> the generally accepted rule is pink for the boy and blue for the girl. The reason is that pink being a more decided and stronger colour, is more suitable for the boy; while blue, which is more delicate and dainty is prettier for the girl.

Another reasoning put forward opined that pink, being a derivative of red, represented a strong, manly colour, while blue was associated with the gentleness of the Virgin Mary.

Eventually, without there being any clear directive or signpost in the zeitgeist, there came a reversal — nobody is sure why. So pink for girls and blue for boys became a *new* tradition ... and the older practice was viewed with some incredulity.

## Dove of peace

*The dove is a symbol of peace.*

Yes, it is — but real doves are not always peaceful.

Within the Judaeo-Christian religions, the association between a dove symbolising good news appears to go back to Noah, who after 40 days of rain sent a dove out to reconnoitre the surrounding devastation. According to the King James Bible, the dove came back carrying in its beak *one single olive leaf* (Genesis 8:11). Over centuries this olive leaf has become 'mis-remembered' as a branch (helped along perhaps by St Jerome's Bible which deliberately decided to render the incident — in Latin — with 'branch' rather than 'leaf').

There is no mention in the Bible of the dove or the olive leaf symbolising anything specific. Because of its association with calm after a storm, the olive leaf or 'branch' came to represent rapprochement after disagreement — burying a hatchet after an argument.

But there are other cultures — Egyptian, Chinese, Greek, Roman — going back many centuries, in which doves are found representing peace, long life, innocence and devotion. So with or without leaf or branch, doves slowly became associated almost universally with the concept of peace and pacifism. Doves appear in political cartoons, on banners and signs at events promoting peace (such as the Olympic Games), and in pacifist literature. A person who is a pacifist is sometimes referred to as a 'dove' — in American politics, a person who advocates diplomacy rather than the use of military resources is often referred to in this way — where 'dove' can even sometimes be semi-pejorative.

In the computer age, a dove and olive-twig fly peacefully across the screen when *Windows Home Premium* 7 opens. And in Christian iconography, beyond being just Noah's messenger, the dove gained a more elevated role, often representing the Holy Spirit of God.

However, in real life, doves are capable of manifesting behaviour quite contrary to peace. Amongst themselves they can be quite aggressive. When doves feel proprietorial about a 'territory' — especially during nesting time — any intrusion will get puffed-up necks and an arrogant attack mode. At a communal suburban feeder, pity help any other breed of bird which tries to muscle in. During the wooing prior to the mating season, if a rival casts eyes in the wrong direction, then gentle dove romance is replaced by dire threats and warnings. And in an aviary, doves in a bad mood can injure and kill weaker birds.

Comfort may be found in referring to those seen behaving aggressively as 'pigeons', because doves and pigeons are the same thing — both are species within the family *Columbidae*, and there is no scientific difference between them. And although variations in colour and size are apparent in the differing species, their names are interchangeable. Custom and usage tend to refer to pigeons which are white — regardless of their size — as 'doves'. But their being white doesn't make them always peaceful.

## Lizzie Borden

*Lizzie Borden took an axe, and gave her mother 40 whacks.*
*When she saw what she had done, she gave her father 41.*

In 1892, Andrew Borden of Fall River, Massachusetts, was a prosperous merchant and bank president, earlier widowed but now remarried, with two grown-up daughters, Lizzie and Emma, from his late wife. On 4 August, while daughter Emma was out-of-town, Andrew Borden and (second) wife Abby were found murdered most viciously, by many axe blows.

Lizzie was arrested and tried, launching an enormously publicised trial. The trial unearthed continually confusing evidence which the public tended to ignore, having decided in advance that Lizzie — who was known to be somewhat at odds with her parents — had done it. Lizzie's distress that her father had recently killed off her pet pigeons was talked about, and that she continued to address her stepmother as 'Mrs Borden'.

The public was so convinced that Lizzie *must* have done it, that there arose a jaunty rhyme announcing that she'd given '40 whacks'. The couplet can still be heard 120 years later, which is somewhat unfair, because what actually happened at the trial was that the jury acquitted Lizzie Borden and declared her not guilty.

## Thumbs up

*Thumbs up meant ancient Roman gladiators were reprieved from further fighting, and thumbs down meant they were to be killed.*

Thumbs up or down have various significances in current times and in different cultures. In many places the upright thumb indicates approval, triumph, excellence, success. In some counties it indicates 'thank you', and many places accept it as a signal from someone who is walking but would be grateful for a vehicle ride. There are cultures where in the rural context an upraised thumb indicates 'male' (the upright smallest finger indicating 'female').

But when travelling in unfamiliar territories, it is prudent to be aware that the perceived significance of hand gestures is not necessarily the same as it is on home territory — and can go astray. In some areas of the Middle East, Africa and South America, the otherwise innocent upward thumb is perceived as a gross sexual insult.

As for ancient Rome, Anthony P. Corbeill, Associate Professor of Classics at Kansas University, has undertaken extensive study in the significance of ancient hand signals. Detailed research in Italy in 1994–95 (after he won the Rome Prize), and further work throughout Europe, helped him track down the 'intended message' given to the historic gladiators at a crucial point of their bout.

His research showed that in ancient Rome, far from being a sign of approval, the 'thumb-up' signal meant 'kill'. And it wasn't static: the thumb-up was in motion upwards (sometimes interpreted as 'stabbing', signifying that the sword should be then thrust up into the opponent's heart). On the other hand, if the crowd's wish was that a gladiator's life be spared, the signal would be a closed fist with the thumb hidden.

Professor Corbeill points out that in ancient gladiatorial signalling, the thumb-up signal in fact conveyed exactly the opposite to its common modern counterparts. He explains that over later centuries a different use of thumb-up has developed, indicating: thumbs up — everything is OK; thumbs down — things are *not* OK.

Attributing these later meanings to be of American development, Corbeill says: 'We confuse the American thumbs-up gesture with the Italian one and mistake the meaning of the audience at gladiatorial contests.'

So the modern thumbs-up (indicating that everything is OK) is precisely the opposite of the ancient thumbs-up (indicating the thrust of doom).

## Plant names

*Many parents name their children after plants.*

Parents of daughters do. Many women are named after flowers and plants, but in an English-speaking culture men very seldom are. Exceptions which could be nominated are Basil, and Rowan (which fits either gender) and at a pinch Forrest (but only with two 'r's).

## Big Ben

*Big Ben is the clock in Westminster Tower.*

It's not the clock; it's the giant bell which chimes the hour. The tower rising from the Palace of Westminster (aka the Houses of

Parliament) was sometimes called St Stephen's Tower, but was re-named Elizabeth Tower in honour of the diamond jubilee of Queen Elizabeth II.

The clock has no actual name, nor have the 'chime bells' any names. But the big bell which announces the number of hours is known as Big Ben. It was cast in 1858 and took 18 hours to haul up into the belfry, where in 1859 it gave its first chime signalling the hour. The origin of the name Big Ben is unclear. It is thought to have been nicknamed after either Sir Benjamin Hall (Commissioner of Works at the time) or perhaps celebrity heavyweight champion Benjamin Caunt.

## The Declaration of Independence

*The American Declaration of Independence was signed on 4 July 1776.*

The Declaration was a document formally declaring independence from Great Britain. The Second Continental Congress ratified the text on 4 July — but it wasn't signed until 2 August.

## Swastika

*Many people think the swastika is a symbol of evil.*

For a certain period of modern history, it was. But that was an aberration in the swastika's long centuries of association with much more positive values.

The name we use for the symbol — 'swastika' — is derived from the Sanskrit language, and means 'well-being' or 'good luck'. In some contexts, the symbol is referred to as the 'hooked cross'.

Use of the swastika symbol was traced by archaeologist Heinrich Schliemann (in 1873) back to the civilisation known as Troy — thus c.1500 BC. Further detailed work by Washington Nation Museum curator Thomas Wilson in 1894 reported the swastika symbol occurring in Mesopotamia and India several thousand years BC, as well as often appearing on objects from ancient Greece. And religious researcher Reverend Norman Walker reported its being found in Japan, China, Manchuria, Korea, Egypt, Armenia, the Caucasus and Scandinavia.

The familiar swastika 'arms' were either right-bending or left-bending, without any particular significance in being so, and sometimes also had an extra 'short arm' midway on each shaft — pointing the same way as the left or right top branch. At times the swastika has symbolised light, lightning, water, and gods Brahma, Vishnu, Shiva, Jupiter and Thor. And in all cases the symbol was associated with sacred goodwill. Thomas Wilson analysed: 'The swastika was always a charm or amulet, a sign of benediction, blessing, long life, fortune, and good luck.'

In 1810, a gymnast in Prussia, F. Ludwig Jahn, featured a swastika-like symbol as a badge for his tramping and gymnastic clubs. He used the variation which had the small out-branch halfway up each shaft, which therefore slightly resembled four 'F's, from which he created a motto intended to inspire German youth: *Frisch, Fromm, Fröhlich, Frei* — fresh, pious, merry and free. But for many people in the following century, the symbol turned out to be anything but those things.

Jahn's double-pronged right-facing swastika gradually became adapted and adopted as a symbol for the Nazi party — purporting to be a symbol of German-ness, and, by mistaken association, Aryan-ness. Mistaken, in that the swastika had for thousands of years been associated with countless non-Aryan cultures.

Its later incorporation into the State flag of Germany, and subsequent events involving that nation, stigmatised the swastika's centuries-old association with reverence and well-being. So, although the swastika is not and never should have been a 'symbol of evil', it does retain that connotation for anyone with connections to Europe, from 1920 and the decades following.

The swastika was also employed in commerce. The Danish-based Carlsberg company began producing beer in 1847 and

gradually became internationally famous. Its early company logos were either an elephant or a swastika. The latter was discontinued in the 1930s because of its growing political symbolism.

## Atlas

*Atlases are called after the Greek god Atlas, who held the world on his shoulders.*

Yes they are, but Atlas didn't hold up the world.

In legend, Atlas sided with the Titans in a war against the Olympians. The Titans didn't win, so the god Zeus, ruler of the Olympians, issued a stern punishment to Atlas. He was banished to the western edge of the Earth to hold the 'heavens and skies' on his shoulders forever, so that Earth and sky would always be separated.

Homer's *Odyssey* (c. eighth century BC) tells: 'And Atlas through hard constraint upholds the wide heaven with unwearying head and arms, standing at the borders of the earth ...'

In later centuries, sculptors attempting to demonstrate the fate of Atlas (for example, the second-century marble statue known as '*Farnese Atlas*') showed him bearing on his shoulders the heavens — the heavens being depicted in the form of a sphere shape covered in celestial symbolism. But because of the 'heavens' being depicted on a solid marble globe, a misconception arose that he was holding up the Earth — disregarding the fact that the idea of the world being 'globe-shaped' was at that time not yet common knowledge.

The confusion became firmer from 1585, when Belgian map-maker Gerardus Mercator published a collection of maps in a book. He didn't call it an 'atlas', but its title page featured an engraving of the legendary Atlas holding a huge globe on his shoulders. This particular globe did not have any depictions on it, either of the Earth or skies, but gradually there began the association of map-books of the Earth's surface with the name Atlas — in tandem with the mistaken image of the god Atlas holding up the world.

But it was the celestial spaces, the heavens, the sky, which Zeus commanded Atlas to carry on his shoulders.

> Even though the legend of Atlas is not perceived as fact, it presents a difficult prospect to figure out, namely: in order to carry the whole world or the whole sky on his shoulders, where would Atlas stand?

# Eros

*A statue of Eros, the Greek god of Love, stands in Piccadilly Circus.*

No. This is a case of confusion between two brothers.

The monument in Piccadilly Circus is officially the Shaftesbury Memorial, in honour of philanthropic Lord Shaftesbury, an admired politician of the nineteenth century. In 1893, sculptor Alfred Gilbert's winged statue was first seen atop the monument. The statue was the first in the world to be cast in aluminium.

Gilbert wanted a subject to signify the unselfish interest and support that Lord Shaftesbury demonstrated, especially to the poor. So he chose the figure of the Greek god of 'selfless requited love'. And that god was Anteros. The choice was quite deliberate. Gilbert is believed to have described his statue as 'portraying reflective and mature love, as opposed to Eros or Cupid, the frivolous tyrant'. But there were problems: most people had never heard of Anteros, who, according to his legend, was the twin brother of Eros, so they looked exactly the same.

Initially, public reaction to the statue and the mistaken perception that it represented Eros (aka Cupid) was perceived as a rather doubtful way of honouring Lord Shaftesbury. So a new name was rapidly dreamed up, and the statue was officially re-designated to be The Angel of Christian Charity. That title has been largely ignored by the populace and visitors, and the correct name Anteros (who, let's face it, has a very low profile in public consciousness) was gradually shortened to just Eros.

It's wrong — but that's the statue's title you'll most often hear.

## Old Mother Shipton

*Old Mother Shipton died in 1561, but she had already predicted email!*

Old Mother Shipton is believed to have been a real person, who, if she existed, died in 1561. Very little is known for certain about her, but legend has her as a prophetess from Yorkshire, who was unattractive to look at, yet somehow made a livelihood predicting events and telling fortunes.

In 1641 — 80 years after she died — a book appeared, purporting to be a collection of her 'predictions'. This caused wide interest; an interest which remained lively for many years. Forty-three years after that first publication, a second edition of her prophesies was printed in 1684, containing hitherto unknown 'facts' about her life, and other 'found' predictions. Interest in her continued through the next century and further.

Another edition emerged in 1862, 300 years after her death, and included some *more* hitherto unseen 'recently found' prophesies. It was this edition in 1862 which featured the two 'prophesies' which made her internationally famous. From approximately 1560, her view into the future appeared to be able to see:

Carriages without horses shall go
And accidents fill the world with woe.
Around the earth thoughts shall fly
In the twinkling of an eye.
Through the hills, men shall ride
And no horse be by his side.
Under water men shall walk,
Shall ride and sleep and also talk.
In the air men shall be seen
In white in black and also green.

Iron in water then shall float
As easily as a wooden boat.
Gold shall be found and shown
In a land that's not now known.

Cars, email, trains, submarines, aeroplanes, ocean liners, and the continent of Australia — Mother Shipton saw them all, supposedly in 1560.

Except that she didn't. The editor and publisher of the 1862 'edition of prophesies', Charles Hindley, under some pointed enquiries, admitted that he had 'created' the 'hitherto unseen prophesies', including the other new one which caused a stir:

The world to an end shall come,
In eighteen hundred and eighty one.

In 1881 when the world didn't come to an end, subsequent emendations professed that she had 'meant' 1981, and when that didn't happen the 'prediction' morphed into 1991.But the world so far has declined to oblige Mr Hindley. And Mother Shipton had nothing to do with it!

Though it has to be admitted that, considering it was fake, thoughts flying around the Earth in the twinkling of an eye wasn't a bad shot for 1862 — since in essence Hindley predicted what we know as cable telegraph, radio, television and the internet.

## Lady Godiva

*Lady Godiva rode naked through the Coventry streets.*

The story might be wishful thinking.

Lady Godiva, Countess of Mercia, was certainly a real person, a wealthy noblewoman living c.1010–1080. The Domesday Book lists her estates. *The Chronicle* attributed to the monk Florentine (d.1118) writes of the death of her husband, Lord Leofric, buried at Coventry:

> which monastery among other good deeds of his life, he and his wife the noble Countess Godiva, and devoted friend of St Mary Ever-a-Virgin had founded, and amply endowing it with lands of their own patrimony.

Florentine continues with praise of the enrichments the Earl Leofric and Countess Godiva had donated to the monasteries of

Leominster and Wenlock, and those at Chester, Worcester and Evesham Abbey. Not a word about her riding naked anywhere.

That matter of her supposed nude ride was first referred to well over a century after Godiva's death, in Roger of Wendover's *Chronica Flores Historiarum* (1235). It had never been mentioned by anyone in the preceding 155 years, and the fact that Roger borrowed efforts from past writers in his compilation has not earned the respect of later historians.

Since 1235, other writers have added 'details' supposed to have occurred at the event — though they couldn't have been there — if ever the ride had happened. The major 'detail' of which was the sudden addition into the story of 'Peeping Tom', who was supposedly struck blind for peeking through a knot-hole at the nude countess.

This fanciful snippet emerged over 550 years after Lady Godiva died — when antiquarian William Camden visited Coventry (1659) and saw a statue of a man with a blank stare and was told that it represented a tailor named Tom who had been struck blind. With no evidence at all, Camden grafted this onto the Godiva-naked-ride myth, and it was taken up by historian Paul de Rapin (1732) and has become an indelible part of the Godiva story.

But there is not a shred of evidence that any of it ever happened.

# Jury

> *There are always 12 people*
> *on a jury.*

Not necessarily so ... it depends on where you are. Many variations emerge on the '12 good men and true' practice. There are not 12 in Scotland, Germany, Hong Kong, Samoa, Italy, Norway and Spain. And in some states of the United States certain cases can assemble a 'grand jury' numbering up to 23 people. And there are countries which don't have a jury at all.

What is not clear is: in those areas which remain with 12, why has it become a practice that guilt or innocence on the facts presented is decided by a group numbering 12? Why *12?* There is no precise explanation available — the background is uncertain.

Belief that the original significance of 12 making a just decision is based on a biblical precedent has been assigned to the Welsh King Morgan, King of Glamorgan (AD 725), of whom it was reported:

> He made a Law that all men who had Lawsuits & quarrels should before they would try them by the law of the land, refer the matter to 12 pious merciful men and the King to be their director. This Law was called the apostolic Law because the King & his twelve elders acted in the manner of Christ & his apostles, that is by mercy and gentleness.

Cardiff Records, Institute of Historical Research.
Copyright © 2012 University of London & History of Parliament Trust

Senator Paul Rand addressed the American Senate in September 2012:

> In 725 A.D., Morgan of Glamorgan, the Prince of Wales, said for as Christ and his 12 Apostles were to so judge the world, so

human tribunals would be composed of 12 wise men. We have been doing this for hundreds upon hundreds of years.

Then there was King Æthelred in AD 933. The King's *Wantage Code* made mention of a justice system involving judgement by a group of 12:

> and let them swear on holy relics, which shall be placed in their hands, that they will never knowingly accuse an innocent man nor conceal a guilty man.

At that time although the practice of '12' was settling in, the word 'jury' was not yet used. In the ancient circumstances of 'trial by group' the word scholars use is 'compurgators'. 'Jury' didn't come into the English language until 300 years later.

But from 1066 onwards, William the Conqueror followed a form of Glamorgan's system, by creating groups of 12 men to assess exact ownership of lands, and to settle civil issues. After that, in the reign of Henry II (1154–1189), groups of 12 'good and lawful men' were used to assess either criminal or civil matters.

And by the time of King John, the Magna Carta decreed (1215):

> All evil customs concerning forests, warrens, and foresters, warreners, sheriffs, and their officers, rivers and their keepers, shall forthwith be inquired into in each county, by twelve knights of the same shire, chosen by the most creditable persons in the same county.

But beliefs in the origin of the modern jury operation are not unanimous. There are other indications that it arose from a Scandinavian system, or from the Islamic *lafif*, which the Normans may have brought from Sicily. Another theory indicates an influence from ancient Germany.

And besides the apostles, there are other significances to the figure 12: King Morgan's relating that the assembly be based on a Christian precedent is not seen universally as the reason for that number. (Besides, he seemed to overlook the fact that while there were 11 faithful, there was one Judas.) Other interpretations of 'why 12?' have some claim, although still associated with biblical references, including: the 12 thrones judging the 12 tribes of Israel (Matthew 19:28), and the 12 legions of angels (Matthew 26:53).

But the number 12 has other resonances. King Arthur's legendary 'Round Table' seated 12; the day is traditionally divided into 12 hours each of day and night, and the year into 12 months; and Christians celebrate the 12 days of Christmas. Britain had a long affinity with very familiar sets of 12: coinage (12 pennies to a shilling) and measure (12 inches to a foot.)

Also, traditionally there are 12 astrological signs of the zodiac, giving rise to a belief held by some that originally the 12 chosen to consider judgement were each of a different zodiac birth sign, thus supposedly giving a complete coverage of human character types.

So there is no indisputable fact, only theories, about why a court trial decision can be settled by a group of 12. For a solution to that question ... the jury is still out.

## Whistler's Mother

Whistler's Mother *is the title of Whistler's most famous painting.*

It probably was his most famous, but while the painting is often referred to as *Whistler's Mother*, that is not the name he gave it.

The painting is a side view of an elderly woman sitting, wearing a floor-length black dress and pale grey diaphanous head-scarf. It was first exhibited in London in 1872 with the title *Arrangement in Grey and Black No. 1.* But London audiences, imbued with Victorian niceties, were uncomfortable with the word 'arrangement' to describe what was clearly a 'portrait' — and a portrait of a woman at that. The name seemed to be something of a dismissal. So a subtitle was added: *Portrait of the Artist's Mother.* Over time and popular usage, the original title plus the addition colloquially became just 'Whistler's Mother'.

But the painting itself (now in the Musée d'Orsay in Paris) is still officially named *Arrangement in Grey and Black No. 1: Portrait of the Artist's Mother.*

## Cinderella's slipper

*Cinderella's slipper was made of glass — or was it fur?*

This has been disputed for years. The earliest known version of the 'Cinderella story' is in ninth-century China, from the book *Miscellaneous Morsels from Youyang* — and the story there is acknowledged as being a much older folk tale.

The maiden Yeh-Hsien is treated cruelly by a bad-tempered stepmother and her ugly daughter, who let her wear only scruffy clothes. But Yeh-Hsien by magic is given a lovely gown to attend a festival — where she loses one golden shoe. The wealthiest merchant in the district finds the shoe and searches for the woman who perfectly fits it. Shoe united at last with Yeh-Hsien, the merchant marries her — and an avalanche of rocks falls on the stepmother and the ugly step-sister.

Since that early publication, several dozen variations on the same theme have surfaced over the centuries, notably in Naples (as 'Zezolla') and Scotland ('Rashin Coatie'), besides other versions in India and Japan. In France, Charles Perrault re-told whatever version he had come across, and *Cendrillon* was published in 1697, and it is this version which has become the most famous and familiar.

Nearly all (of several dozen) versions, including Perrault's, feature the step-sisters' anxiety to fit the 'slipper' which Cinderella dropped — since only a perfect fit will identify the missing young woman. And such is their anxiety that the sisters, or their ambitious mother, do not hesitate to cut off a bit of heel or some toes, to squeeze into the delicate shoe.

The shoe/slipper emerges in different fabrics in different stories: gold, silk, silver, fur — and glass.

A belief was floated that Perrault actually meant the slipper to be made of fur (*vair*) which was mis-translated into English as glass (*verre*). But Perrault was a renowned language expert, a member of the French Academy and contributor to the Dictionary of the Academy. His seventeenth-century version of the Cinderella story in French makes it clear he intended 'glass'. His version is called *Cendrillon ou La Petite Pantoufle de Verre* (*Cinderella or The Little Glass Slipper*) ... so there is no doubt he meant glass (*verre*) and not fur (*vair*).

Researcher Charles Panati opts for *verre* (glass) being deliberate on Perrault's part: the merit of glass being 'it could not be stretched — and could be seen through'. So any foot inside could be observed not to be forced into shape — or have been knifed into a smaller size! So we can be confident Perrault intended the shoe to be glass and not fur.

However, this leaves two embarrassing questions. If Cinderella's shoe was such a perfect fit, why did it fall off when she left the ball? And when it fell off, why didn't it break?

## Uncle Sam

*Uncle Sam is the fictional symbol of America.*

*Au contraire* ... not fictional at all. Unlike Britain's symbolic John Bull, America's Uncle Sam was a real person: Samuel Wilson, born in 1766. Mr Wilson became experienced in the meat industry. During the 1812 war in the United States, Sam Wilson became responsible for meat supplied to the army. To indicate that supplies of meat were for military use, he marked the crates with the initials 'U.S.' — apparently under the impression this would be understood as 'United States', although that term was not common in 1812.

All his fellow workers customarily addressed him as 'Uncle Sam', and when a government inspector visited he asked a staff member what the initials 'U.S.' stood for. The man replied light-heartedly that it probably meant 'Uncle Sam'.

The appellation grew and spread. Soldiers began referring to their rations as 'coming from Uncle Sam', and imperceptibly there grew an association between the phrase 'Uncle Sam' and the actual nation of America.

By 1820 there was a cartoon of him, which assisted the growing fondness for the avuncular man and the image he manifested. The cartoons continued and became more and more colourfully patriotic. A poster to recruit soldiers showed 'Uncle Sam' in flag-themed clothes with the slogan '*I Want You for U.S. Army*' — and sold over 4 million copies. Although the imagery was looking less and less like the real Samuel Wilson, affection for the benign old man remained firm, and the phrase 'Uncle Sam' became widespread, signifying the nation and government of America. Uncle Sam Wilson was known to be a man of great fairness, reliability and honesty, and those who knew him took very kindly to his being associated with the image of all Americans.

He died in 1854, and his grave is in Troy, New York, where he lived. There is a statue there commemorating him as the original Uncle Sam.

In 1961 the American Congress declared: 'Resolved by the Senate and the House of Representatives that the Congress salutes Uncle Sam Wilson of Troy, New York, as the progenitor of America's National symbol of Uncle Sam.'

# the world of business

## Movers and shakers

*Corporates and financial wizards are the 'movers and shakers'.*

Only recently. In its original use the description applied to quite different types of people. The line comes from a poem from 1874 by English poet Arthur William Edgar O'Shaughnessy. But his 'movers and shakers' were a great distance away from sharebrokers and firebrand politicians:

> We are the music makers,
> We are the dreamers of dreams,
> Wandering by lone sea-breakers,
> And sitting by desolate streams; –
> World-losers and world-forsakers,
> On whom the pale moon gleams:
> We are the movers and shakers
> Of the world forever, it seems.

'Ode' from *Music and Moonlight*

The term is still used to describe those who disturb the even tenor of our lives. But in an era of changing supremacies, the poets and music-makers — upon whom the pale moon gleams — move and shake us rather less than in 1874. In present times there are financial lions, oil barons, wizards of electronics, international economists and media magnates who challenge established laws and morals and draw new battle lines.

So the original meaning of O'Shaughnessy's term has completely changed sides.

## Bowler hats

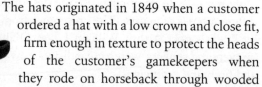

*Bowler hats have that name because they are shaped like a bowl.*

The hats originated in 1849 when a customer ordered a hat with a low crown and close fit, firm enough in texture to protect the heads of the customer's gamekeepers when they rode on horseback through wooded areas. The hatters, Lock & Co. London, placed an order with the makers — T & W Bowler of Southwark – who, naturally enough, put inside each hat their label: Bowler. That's how they became known as 'bowlers'.

## Nerd

*'Nerd' is a new word of the internet era, describing someone immersed in computers.*

Not exactly new. Nowadays a nerd is generally perceived as a person with an almost obsessive interest in a narrow focus of intellectual or technological subject matter, to the exclusion of social graces and activities. But the word long pre-dated computers. It comes from children's author Dr Seuss, in his 1950 story *If I Ran the Zoo*, in which a character proclaims:

... I'll sail to Ka-Troo
And Bring Back an It-Kutch, a Preep and a Proo,
A Nerkle, a Nerd, and a Seersucker, too!

The story was illustrated with a grumpy-looking android clearly not particular about personal grooming.

## Libel and slander

*Libel and slander mean the same thing: you've bad-mouthed someone publicly.*

Not quite, there are shades of difference. Both come under the heading of defamation: making a false and discrediting statement about someone to another person, *other than the person being discredited*. The difference between libel and slander is the form in which the defamatory matter is spread about.

**Libel** refers to publicly circulated false and defamatory statements assailing the character of a person and bringing undeserved discredit by misinformation *in printed words, pictures or other media*.

**Slander** is the utterance and spreading of a false or malicious statement about a person intended to injure or defame, but communicated in a fleeting or transitory form — i.e. *when spoken*.

## Affluent society

*'The affluent society' signifies that most people are now more comfortable than they were in past decades.*

It does signify that now, but that is a major change in its significance since first becoming current in 1958. Canadian-born economist John Kenneth Galbraith had observed the growing prosperous materialism of Americans and their lifestyle:

increasing ownership of luxury cars, multiple
televisions, home appliances, etc.
It was his opinion that many of
these commodities were not
only unnecessary, but also
trivial. He pointed out that
the maintenance and manufacture
of consumer comforts used resources, both
natural and financial, which were pushing the development of
wider public systems — such as schools — into the background.
So he coined the term 'affluent society' as a scornful expression
intended to be ironic — describing those who, motivated by
personal selfishness, reached for unnecessary 'wants' and 'needs'
created by industries such as advertising, whose purpose was to
fill their own pockets by pampering consumers with illusory and
expensive non-necessities.

Over time, Galbraith's scornful term shifted from irony into the
opposite: identifying in a rather complimentary way the fact that
people are living more comfortably than in past decades. 'Affluent
society' is the badge of general prosperity, whether or not the
'public good' has been side-lined.

> Roman historian Cornelius Tacitus in AD 115 had his own version
> of prosperity: 'Many who seem to be struggling with adversity
> are happy; many, amid great affluence, are utterly miserable.'

## Minutes of a meeting

*The 'minutes' of a meeting are a record of
how long it lasted.*

Not at all. The term 'minutes' of a meeting is related to the other
version of the word 'minute' and 'minutiae', meaning 'small'.

French historical expert on civil law Charles Toullier (1845)
explained that minutes are so called because in earlier times notes

of what happened at meetings were kept in a fast-moving, note-taking style known by the Latin *minuta scriptura*, which in modern terms is sometimes translated as 'rough copy' but more formally as 'a draft in abbreviated writing'. The notes were later expanded into full-size writing and reportage on everything which had happened at the meeting, and then distributed. From the Latin *minuta scriptura* came the name 'minutes' for quickly written but detailed, precise notes recording the events and discussion of a meeting.

## Piggy banks

*They're called 'piggy banks' because they look like little pigs.*

They do look like pigs now, because they're made to look that way. But the porcine money-boxes didn't start out like that.

For several centuries in England, a kind of easily found dense orange-coloured clay was called 'pygg' and was much less costly than metal. Industrial physicist and former science editor of *Newsweek* Charles Panati explains in *The Extraordinary Origin of Everyday Things*:

> It was used for making dishes, pots, cups and jars, and the earthenware items were referred to as 'pygg.' Frugal people then, as now, saved cash in kitchen pots and jars.
>
> A 'pygg jar' was not yet shaped like a pig — but the name persisted and the clay was forgotten.

Potters with a rotund lump of clay had started to fashion the lump into the likeness of a miniature pig — made from 'pygg'. The pig-shape made from pygg became a firm favourite for coin-storing, while the name of the clay slowly slipped out of use.

## Model T Ford

*Henry Ford said 'They can have any colour
so long as it's black.'*

More or less. His 1922 autobiography, *My Life and Work*, puts it
slightly differently:

Therefore in 1909 I announced one morning, without any
previous warning, that in the future we were going to build only
one model, that the model was going to be 'Model T,' and that
the chassis would be exactly the same for all cars, and I remarked:
'Any customer can have a car painted any colour that he wants so
long as it is black.'

# good sports

## Golf

*The word 'golf' is an abbreviation of 'Gentlemen Only, Ladies Forbidden'.*

This is a total myth. The ancestor of the word 'golf' was first seen in 1457 as 'gouf' — described then by the Scottish Parliament as a 'forbidden game' because it distracted players from more purposeful military pursuits such as archery.

In Scotland, 'gouf' (sometimes seen as 'gowf') had the meaning of 'to strike'. The origin of the word is not clear; scholars believe it to have developed as a variation on the Dutch word *kolf*, meaning 'a bat or club'. But even the *Oxford English Dictionary* is not definite about this, cautiously ascribing the old Dutch word *kolf* as the 'probable' ancestor of the Scottish word 'gouf' — hence 'golf'.

But not 'Gentleman Only, Ladies Forbidden'.

## World Series

*No other countries take part in America's so-called 'World Series' of baseball.*

Actually, one team from Canada is permitted to participate in the contest. Apart from that, all the teams participating are American, so the inclusion of one non-national team makes only a small dent in the surprisingly narrow focus of announcing a 'World Series' which has no participation from the rest of the world's nations.

The phenomenon began in 1903, known then as World's Championship Series, gently morphing in World Championship Series (no apostrophe 's'), and then just World Series — which appeared in the *Spalding Guide* from 1917 onwards. (A rumour arose that the use of the word 'World' had been because of a sponsorship from the *New York World* newspaper, but this was firmly debunked by the Baseball Hall of Fame.)

There is an unavoidable impression that a single nation mounting an internal 'World' championship series, the winners of which are proclaimed World Champions, is a prime form of hubris.

When queried, the usual explanation from an American is that their professional Major League Baseball teams taking part in the 'World Series' contain many players recruited from other countries, such as Mexico, the Dominican Republic, Japan, Taiwan, Cuba, and so on. So the championship is *involving* the best players in the world. This engenders a confusing supposition that, since the best talent found in foreign parts is actually playing in America as part of an American team, these so-called 'American' teams are somehow also playing *on behalf of* Mexico, Japan, Taiwan, etc. — which of course is not the case.

Curiously, such an explanation does not apply when players from another country are 'poached' into national teams of rugby union, rugby league or association football.

## William Webb Ellis

*William Webb Ellis invented the game of rugby.*

The name William Webb Ellis as the avowed 'inventor' of rugby union, slowly became akin to the holy grail. But the belief in his participation (if any) has more holes in it than Swiss cheese, and as many versions as whether Eve ate an apple, a fig, a pomegranate, grapes or a pear.

Almost anyone interested in rugby, anywhere in the world, knows the legend: how in the 1820s teenager William Webb Ellis, during a game at Rugby school, picked up the ball and — shock, horror — *ran forward still holding it* ... which was distinctly against the rules at the time. Alas, examining the 'legend' and its supposed sources shows that it doesn't stand up to even 10 minutes of consideration, and reveals that it is a myth.

How did the legend arise?

In 1876, four years after Webb Ellis had died, out of the blue came a man called Matthew Bloxham (who had never met Webb Ellis). Without naming any source or witnesses, Bloxham wrote about Webb Ellis and the 'picking the ball up and running' incident which had supposedly happened over 50 years earlier in 1824. This was never questioned, although nobody who was ever at school with Webb Ellis had mentioned such an incident — and by 1876 many were dead anyway. Four years after his first shining a doubtful light on Webb Ellis, Bloxham wrote about the hearsay incident a second time — now revising the 'remembered date' to 1823. Nearly a decade on, in 1889, Bloxham's own book, *Rugby — the School*, revised Webb Ellis's 'hold-and-run' date *again* — to 1825.

Out of these three totally unverified and inconsistent reports, a major sporting legend grew. (Matthew Bloxham was perhaps the inspiration for one of Clive James's quixotic titles: *Unreliable Memoirs*.)

Rugby historian Derek Robinson points out that there is not a shred of evidence that the 'incident' ever happened. During Webb Ellis's lifetime, there is no known recalling of his legendary run with the ball at school. He later went to Oxford and played cricket; no report exists of his having any interest in rugby football. He became a clergyman and died in France aged 66, in 1872. By then, the Rugby Football Union had been formed, international matches were being played — and not a word of Webb Ellis had ever been mentioned.

Diligent searching has never uncovered any shred of evidence from anybody who actually witnessed the incident. Thomas Hughes, author of *Tom Brown's School Days*, was at Rugby school seven years after Webb Ellis left, but Hughes said he had never heard of Webb Ellis as a footballer, adding that any 'Webb Ellis tradition had not survived to my day'.

Webb Ellis's connection with rugby, and the year in which it did or did not occur, have to be viewed as somewhat ephemeral. In 2006, the International Rugby Board stated its opinion of Bloxham as 'having undermined his credibility'.

Sports tend to arise through a slow process of evolution rather than a single specific incident. Derek Robinson points out that 'Most games were not invented — they just evolved.'

But the public often prefers a legend to the truth. And this legend remains in two very tangible forms: the plaque at Rugby School commemorating what (might have) happened; and the prestigious and hotly contended competitive trophy in world rugby, called … the Webb Ellis Cup.

But it has been said of the Webb Ellis legend that it has more gaps than a disorganised rugby back line.

Webb Ellis was buried in Menton in 1872, unnoticed until 1958. After his burial place was identified, the French Rugby Federation renovated the (somewhat dilapidated) grave. Despite the 'legend' being now discounted as a myth, Webb Ellis's grave has four separate plaques identifying that he 'took the ball in his hands and ran with it, in 1823'. To honour the legend, Menton has erected a walking trail of 25 'Webb Ellis' rugby-themed panels, starting at the railway station and leading to the cemetery.

## Baseball

*Baseball originated in America.*

Maybe. There is no question that the sophisticated and highly organised version of the sport now popular in the United States was *developed* there. But earlier (and simpler) manifestations were known and named in Britain, before the game surfaced in America (1791).

The first known mention of the game in print is in English publisher John Newberry's 1744 *Little Pretty Pocket Book*:

Base-ball —
'The ball once struck off, Away flies the boy...
To the next destined post — and then Home with joy!'

In the 1700s the royal family in Britain was acquainted with the game and the name — in 1748 Baroness Hervey wrote that the Prince of Wales's children were 'diverting themselves with baseball, a play all who are or have been schoolboys, are well acquainted with'.

English lawyer William Bray as a teenager recorded in his 1755 diary:

Easter Monday, March 31st: Went to Stoke church this morn. After dinner, went to Miss Jeale's to play at base ball with her, the 3 Miss Whiteheads, Miss Billinghurst, Miss Molly Flutter, Mr. Chandler, Mr. Ford and H. Parsons. Drank tea and stayed til 8.

Jane Austen was also clearly familiar with the game, and assumed her readers would be, too, giving it a passing mention in *Northanger Abbey* (1798) during its 'hyphen' phase:

It was not very wonderful that Catherine, who had nothing heroic about her, should prefer cricket, base-ball, riding on horseback, and running about the country ...

The term 'base ball' used by Mr Bray and 'baseball' by Lady Hervey are some of the related names and variations by which the English 'folk game' was played, involving a bat, a ball, running and bases. Over decades and various places, the names varied: base ball; goal ball; round ball; fletch-catch; stool ball; and, simply, base. All of them seemed to be affiliated with a game also known as 'rounders'.

The light afternoon frolic at the Stoke church in 1755 and later Jane Austen's tomboy Catherine show that folksy beginnings of the game were long familiar in England. Those folksy beginnings underwent major developments to become the fast, furious and fiercely competitive sport which developed in America in the late 1700s.

Direct evidence of whether the British 'base-ball' sailed with the Pilgrim Fathers and took on a new coat in the new land has never been established.

## Ping-pong

*'Ping-pong' is a Chinese game.*

'Ping-pong' is a British game, not Chinese — and correctly, it should be referred to as 'table tennis'.

The game arose as a pastime during the late 1800s, believed to have originated among British military officers serving overseas. Each man, with a cigar-box lid in hand, batted a golf ball (or a champagne cork) to and fro over a pile of books laid across a table. It caught on to a certain extent back home, as an after-dinner pastime before television was invented.

Seeing a commercial opportunity, some versions of the game were manufactured for sale — named as 'Wiff Waff' or 'Gossima', based on the unique sound of the game's bats and bouncing balls.

In 1901 the name 'Ping-Pong' was trademarked by J. Jaques & Son Ltd, who onsold the trademark to Parker Brother USA for use of the name in America. All other manufacturers had to use the name 'table tennis'. Again, the name was based on the 'ping' of the bat hitting the ball, and the 'pong' of the ball hitting the table.

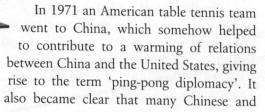

In 1971 an American table tennis team went to China, which somehow helped to contribute to a warming of relations between China and the United States, giving rise to the term 'ping-pong diplomacy'. It also became clear that many Chinese and

Japanese people were particularly good at table tennis, so a vague legend arose that the game and the name originated in China.

In Puccini's opera *Turandot*, first staged in 1926, the three senior courtiers at the Emperor of China's court are called Ping, Pang and Pong. The names just sound Oriental!

All of the above happened before 1930, so the words were fairly well established before radar began using the term 'ping' for a radar signal, and before computers started using the word 'ping' to indicate that a message needs a reply, and then 'pong' when the return message has been activated.

## Olympic Games

*The first 'modern' Olympic Games were held in Athens in 1896.*

Those games were beaten three decades earlier by the 'Olympian Association' in the British town of Much Wenlock, Shropshire. An Olympian Society was formed there by Dr William Brookes, and Olympic Games were held in Shropshire in 1861. They went national in 1866 and were moved to London.

Baron de Courbertin was inspired by the example. So he visited Shropshire and appointed Dr Brookes as honorary delegate to the 1894 Sorbonne Conference. This conference launched the International Olympic Committee, leading to the Athens event in 1896, 30 years after Much Wenlock, Shropshire, had re-activated the ancient Olympic spirit.

Even earlier than Much Wenlock, 'Olympick Games' were being held in the Cotswold village of Chipping Camden from 1612 onwards. Styled as 'village Olympics', the event includes running, jumping, horse-racing, hounds coursing, sledge-hammer throwing, fighting with swords and cudgels, wrestling, dancing ... plus chess, cards and shin-kicking!

# of coronets and kings

## Henry VIII

*King Henry VIII was married six times.*

Maybe not — it depends who you ask. According to the Pope, he was married only once: to his widowed sister-in-law, the Spanish Princess Catherine of Aragon. When Catherine produced only a daughter, Henry's pique at the Pope refusing to annul the marriage caused Henry himself to declare it 'annulled' — on the grounds that she had previously been married to his own brother, which made her second wedding illegal. (However, Catherine's first husband had died several years before, and it wasn't illegal to marry a widow.)

Having done the annulling himself and discarded the authority of the Pope, Henry appointed himself Head of the new Church of England, and allowed that, since he had 'annulled' Catherine, he was free to marry Anne Boleyn.

Queen Anne Boleyn produced the baby Elizabeth, and the marriage lasted until the King's eye was caught by Jane Seymour, and Anne became an inconvenience. So on 17 May 1536 Henry caused it to be announced that his marriage to Anne Boleyn was annulled — made null and void because of supposed adultery and 'witchcraft'. Then two days later an execution made her even more null and void.

After a discreet wait of 11 days, Henry then married Jane Seymour — in what Henry would have considered his 'first' marriage, since the previous two were annulled. Queen Jane provided Henry with his only legitimate male heir (later King Edward VI), but died in doing so, leaving Henry widowed.

The next candidate was from Germany: Lady Anne, daughter of the Duke of Cleves. Wooed by a too-flattering portrait of her, plus a welcome alliance with a German state, Henry discovered on actually meeting her that the portrait and the lady didn't match very well, but he went through the wedding ceremony anyway. However, the marriage was never consummated, which gave good reason for — yes, another annulment.

This left Henry 'legally free' to marry Catherine Howard. Within two years he discovered she was guilty of 'indiscretions' sufficient for her to be beheaded — although they were still married. Henry was widowed again.

Never one to be frugal, Henry cast an eye on Catherine Parr — who herself had been widowed twice before they met. But marry they did, and she was the only one to outlive him and still be Queen at the time.

So King Henry was never actually divorced. Three of Henry's marriages were annulled: to Catherine of Aragon, Anne Boleyn and Anne of Cleves. Quite different from divorce, the meaning of the term 'annulled' is that they had never been 'true marriages' and could be considered *not to have taken place at all.*

His marriage to Jane Seymour ended when she died (naturally), leaving him widowed, while his next marriage, to Catherine Howard, ended with her beheading while still Queen, so Henry was widowed a second time, then married Catherine Parr — and she outlived him.

Three annulments, twice widowed, once outlived ... but without any divorcing!

So how many times did Henry VIII 'marry'? The Catholic Church would say 'only once married', because the three annulments were not decreed by the Pope. Putting aside the Pope's point of view, the tally could be three, since he was 'legally single' after the three annulments declared by the Supreme Head of the Church of England — himself — when he married Catherine Howard. She and his next wife both died while he was still married to them, and his last wife outlived him.

The complications of defining 'married' to suit everyone from Catherine of Aragon onwards make the question much simpler, if re-worded. Namely: 'How many *weddings* did Henry VIII have?'

Answer: six.

## Queen Victoria

*Queen Victoria was not amused.*

Although often 'quoted' confidently as evidence of Victoria's dourness and restrictive attitude towards anyone else's fun, the truth is that there is absolutely zero evidence that she ever made that remark.

The rumour surfaced in a New Zealand newspaper in 1895 which described an incident where the Queen had declared herself 'not amused'. However, while assuring readers the story was 'perfectly true', significantly the writer admitted merely reporting *what someone else had 'told' someone else*.

Twenty-four years later another version emerged in a book published anonymously: *Notebooks of a Spinster Lady* (1919). This report from the 'spinster lady' also cannot be taken seriously. Because:

the so-called 'quote' was published 18 years after Queen Victoria died, so the author didn't hear Victoria say it,

the so-called incident is introduced with the ominous words 'there is a tale ...'

no identity is given to the person who supposedly told the tale, and the book's author, identified as Caroline Holland, was herself dead when the book appeared, so further verification couldn't be sought.

Queen Victoria's last surviving grand-daughter, Princess Alice of Athlone, was interviewed by BBC television in 1976 when she was an intelligently articulate 93. She explained that she once asked her grandmother about the 'not amused' matter, and the Queen replied that 'she'd never said it'.

But there is little difficulty in establishing that in fact Queen Victoria was often quite willing to be amused. After a visit to Paris she wrote to her uncle the King of the Belgians that she had been 'delighted, enchanted, amused and interested'.

In her 1999 biography of Victoria, eminent historian Elizabeth Countess Longford (who was given access to all the Queen's letters and papers) says the legendary 'We are not amused' is pure invention. Lady Longford points out that, on the contrary, the Queen's writings often contained the line 'I was much amused.'

## The King of Siam

*The King of Siam was bald.*

He wasn't. The real King Rama IV (Mongkut) (right) had plenty of hair, and so did Rex Harrison as the King in the 1946 movie *Anna and the King of Siam*. Yul Brynner had plenty of hair too (he shaved his head every day). But playing the King as bald, and other liberties taken with the musical and movie, *The King and I*, were so considerable that the background reality was virtually abandoned.

The real Anna Leonowens was a 31-year-old widow when she went to work for the 58-year-old King, who had numerous wives, and 67 royal children (the count moved up to 82 before his death). The wives all lived with female relatives, slaves and servants, in a totally enclosed territory which held 9000 women.

When *The King and I* musical opened on Broadway in 1951, Thai people were aghast with disbelief at how Anna was depicted (by Gertrude Lawrence) as continually insulting her employer's royal status. She sang: 'I come from a civilised land called Wales, where men like you are kept in county jails.' This blatant impertinence towards a monarch did not go down at all well with Thais.

What is political correctness? Nineteenth-century Siamese people believed in the axiom: 'Better a sword be thrust through thy mouth than that thou utter a word against him who ruleth.' To them *that* was politically correct.

## Marie Antoinette

*Marie Antoinette said those without bread could 'eat cake'.*

There is absolutely no evidence that Marie Antoinette said it. The line had been a familiar expression long before she arrived in France. It appears in the section of Jean-Jacques Rousseau's *Confessions* written in 1765 — where he attributed the line to 'a great princess', but didn't say which one. At that time, Marie Antoinette was a princess — but only 10 years old, still living in Austria, and had never yet been to France.

Rousseau's account did not say 'cake' but 'brioche' — a bun-shaped baked item of slightly sweet soft pastry, superior to bread as its mix contains eggs and butter. This has been interpreted in English as 'cake'.

There is no contemporary evidence that Marie Antoinette made the remark. She died in 1793 and the claim that she had said 'let them eat brioche' didn't appear until 50 years later. French writer Jean-Baptiste Alphonse Karr (who was born 15 years after Marie Antoinette died), without any evidence at all, brought the world's attention to the supposed 'let them eat cake' quote in his monthly journal *Les Guêpes* (March 1843), which was often satirical in tone.

Although totally without foundation, reports of her saying 'Let them eat brioche' crept into later publications, and became 'folk history'. The line appeared to sum up the selfishness of the French upper classes and their lack of contact with reality.

But the fact remains that no actual report exists that Marie Antoinette ever said it.

## King Canute

*King Canute tried to stop the tide coming in.*

This is historic legend in reverse gear. Canute (King of England 1016, and also King of Denmark and Norway) was by all accounts a formidable ruler and a practical and honest man. The only known account of the King's encounter with the sea was written by the historian Archdeacon Henry of Huntingdon in *Historia Anglorum*, published c.1129, nearly a hundred years after Canute died.

Henry reported that, as a King, Canute 'conducted himself gracefully and magnificently', and that, far from demonstrating delusions of grandeur, he knew very well that commanding Nature was not within a King's power, and created an incident to demonstrate that the sea and its movements were immune to the wishes of any man, King or not. Archdeacon Henry's account (from the original Latin):

> Cnut set his throne by the sea shore and commanded the tide to halt and not wet his feet and robes. Yet continuing to rise as usual the tide dashed over his feet and legs without respect to his royal person. Then the king leapt backwards, saying: 'Let all men know how empty and worthless is the power of kings, for there is none worthy of the name, but He whom heaven, earth, and sea obey by eternal laws.'

So it is a distinct reversal of the event to represent that Canute believed he could command the tide to stop — when he was actually demonstrating that he could *not*, and nor could any man, since the frailty of man, even a King, was no match for the greater power of God.

## Nero

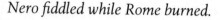

*Nero fiddled while Rome burned.*

This can be dismissed as totally inaccurate, and possibly unfair.

Inaccurate because there was no way Nero could have played a fiddle during the great fire of AD 64. The invention of the fiddle (violin) and its settling down into the form we now recognise didn't happen until 1500 years later. Even his behaviour during the fire, where it was, where he was, what caused it, etc. is presented with many variations which don't fit with each other. One account, by contemporary Tacitus, points out that during the fire Nero wasn't even in Rome, but at a villa in Antium, 30 miles away.

The one thing we can ponder over is that whoever's translation of the events into English used the word 'fiddle' would probably have been more accurate if they'd said 'lyre'. That instrument was available at the time, and Nero was known to be able to play it.

But the accounts, however inaccurate, have left the English language with a very useful expression: 'to fiddle while Rome burns', meaning 'to do nothing or something trivial while knowing that something else disastrous is happening'.

## The people's princess

*The description 'the people's princess' was first used about Diana, Princess of Wales.*

The expression had been used over a century earlier when referring to an earlier British princess: HRH Crown Princess Charlotte Augusta. She was the only legitimate heir to King George IV, and the public delighted in her throughout her short life — truly the 'people's princess'.

When Charlotte died in childbirth in 1817, *The Times* leader wrote: 'We never recollect so strong and general an exhibition and indication of sorrow.' People of every class cried in the streets, memorial services were crowded, and the entire population seemed united in sadness: destitute labourers, the poor and homeless, all wore armbands of black. The Royal Exchange, the Law Courts, and the docks closed — even gambling dens shut down on the day of her funeral.

A hundred and eighty years later, the death of Diana caused a similar outpouring of public grief, and thousands of bouquets were laid at the palace gate. The speechwriter for Prime Minister Tony Blair included Diana (quite rightly) with Charlotte as a 'people's princess'.

> The death of 'the people's princess' Charlotte had a major effect on British history. Her father the King had three brothers, two of whom died without any legitimate children. (Rumour endowed them with 15 illegitimate children between them — but these couldn't inherit the throne.) The third and youngest brother had also died, but he had left a legitimate daughter who somewhat unexpectedly became heir to the throne. She was Princess Alexandrina of Kent, who became the formidable Queen Victoria.

## Annus horribilis

*Queen Elizabeth II invented the term 'annus horribilis'.*

The Queen used the expression during a speech at the Guildhall, referring to the year of 1992, when she experienced the disastrous fire at Windsor Castle, as well as some tense and very public family problems.

The aptness and novelty of the phrase caught immediate attention, and her use of the expression was widely quoted, often attributing the term to Her Majesty herself. But commentators tended to overlook one part of the Queen's speech. She said:

> 1992 is not a year I shall look back on with undiluted pleasure. In the words of *one of my more sympathetic correspondents*, it has turned out to be an *annus horribilis*.

The expression was a modern reversal of the title of a Dryden poem from 1667 '*Annus Mirabilis*' ('Year of Wonders'), and prior to the Queen's speech the *mirabilis* version had been seen occasionally as an expression in newspapers and as the title of a Philip Larkin poem in 1967. But the 'sympathetic correspondent' to whom the Queen referred was Sir Edward Spencer Ford, who in a letter to the Queen reversed the term *annus mirabilis* into *annus horribilis*, which she then quoted. When Sir Edward Spencer Ford died, the *Guardian* described him as the person who gave 'the Queen's worst year in office its Latin tag'.

## Prince Albert

*Queen Victoria's husband Prince Albert introduced Christmas trees to Britain.*

Victoria was accustomed to Christmas trees in England long before she married. Decorated evergreen trees had been part of December celebrations in Continental Europe for many centuries, reminding everyone that cold weather was now heading towards spring. King George III's wife, Queen Charlotte, came to England from Germany, and from 1800 onwards introduced a decorated tree to the British royal family as part of Christmas. Her grand-daughter Victoria was familiar with the December festivities of the royals, including a tree, by the time she was 10, and when she was 13 she had one of her own at Kensington Palace. Later, her German husband, Prince Albert, was of course familiar with the custom, and it became a normal part of their Christmas.

In 1848 Victoria and Prince Albert (who had been married eight years by then) and family were depicted in the *Illustrated London News* standing around a lavishly decorated 'Christmas tree'. Such was the power of royal imagery — particularly Queen Victoria's — that landed gentry, society hostesses, and anyone conscious of trends, took on the 'royal' custom, and soon Britain erupted with domestic Christmas trees ... and much of the world still does.

A fascinating sideline emerged regarding the famous illustration of Victoria and Albert's family with their lavish tree: the picture was reproduced in America, but with every detail indicating royalty removed — no medals, sashes of Orders, tiaras, or Albert's moustache — and the modified version was passed off as 'an American family'.

## Carrots and kings

*Carrots were bred to be orange to honour the Dutch royal family.*

There is no evidence at all that this belief has any basis in fact.

Carrots originate in Afghanistan — and it's true that originally they were a colour close to purple. Selective cultivation over centuries, from the wild into the domestic version, has resulted in carrots being purple, white, yellow — or orange. The World Carrot Museum in Britain points out that European oil paintings of the sixteenth and seventeenth centuries show that carrots had by then become the now-familiar orange colour.

But their colour has no connection with Dutch royalty.

The royal family of the Netherlands takes the name Orange from the town in Provence originally known as Arausio, which used to be a legal adjunct of Holland as a separate principality. For no definitely known reason, the town's name gradually drifted into becoming Orange, and its early ruler, William Nassau-Dillenberg, besides having extensive estates in Holland, became known as the Prince of Orange. The Dutch revolt against the Spanish in 1648 resulted in the independence of Holland, and the title of 'Orange' then gradually moved from Prince to King. The royal family of the Netherlands has held the name and the title 'Orange' ever since. So, too, has the French town — it is still called Orange.

But while there is a connection between the Dutch royals and the French town of Orange, there is no known evidence linking the colour of modern carrots with the Kings and Queens of the Netherlands.

The World Carrot Museum dismisses any connection between the two as 'apocryphal' and a 'myth'. Food historian Dr William Thomas Fernie, in his 1895 book *Herbal Simples Approved for Modern Uses of Cure*, wrote that the early historic situation was actually the reverse:

> The Dutch Government had no love for the House of Orange: and many a grave burgomaster went so far as to banish from his garden the Orange lily, and Marigold; also the sale of Oranges and Carrots was prohibited in the markets on account of their aristocratic colour.

Carrots are no longer banned in the Netherlands, and the Dutch royal family is very popular.

# bibliography

Wherever possible, sources are acknowledged within the text of the appropriate topic. In addition to *Encyclopedia Britannica* and *The Oxford English Dictionary*, sources include:

Elliott, Jock, *Inventing Christmas*, Harry N. Abrams, New York, 2002.

Kruszelnicki, Karl, *Dis Information and Other Wikkid Myths*, Harper Collins, Sydney, 2005.

Moore, Edwin, *Lemmings Don't Leap*. Chambers, Edinburgh, 2006.

O'Conner, Patricia and Kellerman, Stewart, *Origins of the Specious*. Random House, New York, 2009.

O'Connor, Anahad, *Never Shower in a Thunderstorm*. Times Books, New York, 2007.

Panati, Charles, *Extraordinary Origins of Everyday Things*. Harper & Row, New York, 1987.

Partridge, Eric, *Origins*. Book Club Associates, London, 1978.

Robertson, Patrick, *The Shell Book of Firsts*. Michael Joseph, London, 1983.

Room, Adrian, *Placenames of the World*. Angus & Robertson, London, 1974.

**If you enjoyed this book, you will love these other books by Max Cryer:**

*Curious English Words and Phrases: The truth behind the expressions we use.* Informative and entertaining, this is a treasure trove for lovers of language, as Max Cryer dispels myths and uncovers meanings. From 'couch potato' to 'Bob's your uncle', you'll find the explanation here.

*Preposterous Proverbs: Why fine words butter no parsnips.* With his characteristic wry wit, Max Cryer looks at a vast array of proverbs from around the world, analysing the origin and meaning behind some of the most interesting and perplexing proverbs.

*Who Said That First?: The curious origins of common words and phrases.* In this very readable book, Max Cryer explores the origins of hundreds of expressions we use and hear every day – with some surprising findings. Written in his delightfully witty style.

*Every Dog Has Its Day: A thousand things you didn't know about man's best friend.* This superb collection tells the stories of famous dogs, explains the origins of some favourite breeds, describes the surprising activities in which dogs are involved and how dogs have infiltrated our language.

*The Godzone Dictionary: Favourite New Zealand words and phrases.* A concise A-Z dictionary of the words and phrases that make the New Zealand language and speech patterns unique. Kiwis and visitors alike will find this dictionary 'Sweet As'!

*Love Me Tender: The stories behind 40 of the world's favourite songs.* Many of the world's best-loved songs have truly remarkable origins. This book is full of surprises, revealing the fascinating stories behind a range of songs, from 'Amazing Grace' to 'Moon River'.

Love books? Love words? Visit www.wordbooks.com.au

**EXISLE**
PUBLISHING

www.exislepublishing.com